Can You Outsmart a Sunday Schooler?

Conover Swofford

BARBOUR
PUBLISHING

All scripture quotations, unless otherwise noted, are taken from the King James Version of the Bible.

Scripture quotations marked NKJV are taken from the New King James Version®. Copyright © 1982 by Thomas Nelson, Inc. Used by permission. All rights reserved.

Published by Barbour Publishing, Inc., P.O. Box 719, Uhrichsville, Ohio 44683, www.barbourbooks.com

Our mission is to publish and distribute inspirational products offering exceptional value and biblical encouragement to the masses.

 Member of the
Evangelical Christian
Publishers Association

Printed in the United States of America.

Contents

Introduction

So, how well did you listen during Sunday school? Find out with *Can You Outsmart a Sunday Schooler?* This collection of 50 ten-question quizzes will test your knowledge of favorite Bible stories and topics, covering categories like:

- The Acts of the Apostles
- Cities
- Husbands and Wives
- Numbers
- Parables
- The Word of God

Answers follow the tenth question of each quiz.

Scoring

- Answer *eight or more* in each quiz, you've outsmarted the Sunday schoolers.

- Answer *five to seven* questions, you're still in Sunday school.

- Answer *four or fewer* correctly, you need to get to Sunday school. . .fast!

Can You Outsmart a Sunday Schooler?

It doesn't matter to God how old you are.
What matters is that you're willing to serve Him.
Here are some young people in the Bible who God
used in amazing ways. How much do you know
about them?

Question #1

Before Daniel was taken captive to Babylon, he was a:
- a) prince
- b) shepherd
- c) musician
- d) cupbearer

Question #2

Moses' sister who watched over him in his basket in
the river was:
- a) Deborah
- b) Ruth
- c) Esther
- d) Miriam

Question #3

David was the youngest of how many brothers?
- a) 6
- b) 7
- c) 8
- d) 9

Question #4

The Hebrew maid who told her mistress that Elisha could cure leprosy served the wife of:
- a) Jehu
- b) Jehoram
- c) Naaman
- d) Nehemiah

Question #5

Who was thrown into a pit and then sold into slavery by his own brothers?
- a) Reuben
- b) Simeon
- c) Joseph
- d) Benjamin

Question #6

The youngest king of Judah was how old when he began to reign?

- a) 7
- b) 8
- c) 10
- d) 12

Question #7

The second-youngest king of Judah was how old when he began to reign?

- a) 8
- b) 10
- c) 12
- d) 14

Question #8

The boy who gave Jesus his lunch had:
  a) 2 loaves and 5 fish
  b) 3 loaves and 5 fish
  c) 5 loaves and 2 fish
  d) 5 loaves and 3 fish

Question #9

When Samuel was dedicated to God's service, he worked for which priest?
  a) Phinehas
  b) Eli
  c) Abimelech
  d) Melchizedek

Question #10

How old was Jarius's daughter when Jesus raised her from the dead?
  a) 10
  b) 12
  c) 14
  d) 16

Young People in the Bible

ANSWERS

1. a) prince (Daniel 1:3, 6)

2. d) Miriam (Exodus 2:3–4;
   Numbers 26:59)

3. c) 8 (1 Samuel 16:10–11)

4. c) Naaman (2 Kings 5:1–3)

5. c) Joseph (Genesis 37:26–28)

6. a) 7 (2 Kings 11:2–4, 12)

7. a) 8 (2 Kings 22:1)

8. c) 5 loaves and 2 fish (John 6:9)

9. b) Eli (1 Samuel 1:20–25)

10. b) 12 (Luke 8:41–42, 54–55)

Did you outsmart
the Sunday schoolers?

Can You
Outsmart
a
Sunday
Schooler?

By Any Other Name

Sometimes we know a biblical character by one name, but the Bible also gives us another less familiar name for that person. Or we may know biblical characters by their names but not by their titles. How familiar are you with these lesser-known names and titles of famous biblical characters?

Question #1

Esther's Hebrew name was:
- a) Ruth
- b) Deborah
- c) Hadassah
- d) Miriam

Question #2

Belteshazzar was the Babylonian name for:
- a) Jeremiah
- b) Daniel
- c) Ezekiel
- d) Nehemiah

Question #3

Hanaiah's Babylonian name was:
- a) Shadrach
- b) Meshach
- c) Abednego
- d) Nebuchadnezzar

Question #4

Which two disciples did Jesus call
"the sons of thunder"?
- a) Peter and Andrew
- b) James and John
- c) Peter and James
- d) Andrew and John

Question #5

Who was given Zaphnath-paaneah as his
Egyptian name?
- a) Moses
- b) Jacob
- c) Joseph
- d) Benjamin

Question #6

What man in the Bible is specifically referred to as
"the Jews' enemy"?
- a) Pharaoh
- b) Herod
- c) Haman
- d Judas

Question #7

What priest's sons were called "sons of Belial"?
- a) Aaron
- b) Eli
- c) Samuel
- d) Phinehas

Question #8

Whom did Jesus say was the "son of perdition"?
   a) Satan
   b) Herod
   c) Judas
   d) Pilate

Question #9

Of the seven chosen in Acts 6:5, which one was referred to as "the evangelist"?
   a) Stephen
   b) Philip
   c) Nicolas
   d) Timon

Question #10

Whom did Jesus say was the greatest man ever born?
   a) Moses
   b) Abraham
   c) Adam
   d) John the Baptist

By Any Other Name

ANSWERS

1. c) Hadassah (Esther 2:7)
2. b) Daniel (Daniel 1:7)
3. a) Shadrach (Daniel 1:7)
4. b) James and John (Mark 3:17)
5. c) Joseph (Genesis 41:45)
6. c) Haman (Esther 3:10)
7. b) Eli (1 Samuel 2:12)
8. c) Judas (John 17:12; 18:2)
9. b) Philip (Acts 21:8)
10. d) John the Baptist (Matthew 11:11)

Did you outsmart
the Sunday schoolers?

Can You
Outsmart
a
Sunday
Schooler?

Some people in the Bible had some very strange dreams. Sometimes the dream was a vision that needed interpretation. Sometimes God gave specific instructions to someone in a dream. What do you know about these people and their dreams?

Question #1

Jacob dreamed of a _____ that went to heaven.

    a) staircase   c) mountain
    b) ladder   d) chariot

Question #2

Pharaoh dreamed that seven skinny _____ ate seven fat _____.

    a) cattle   c) horses
    b) sheep   d) fish

Question #3

When Nebuchadnezzar dreamed of a strange figure, who interpreted his dream for him?

    a) Babylonian wise men
    b) Joseph
    c) Daniel
    d) astrologers

Question #4

Where were Joseph, the butler, and the baker when Joseph interpreted their dreams for them?
  - a) Pharaoh's palace
  - b) a field
  - c) jail
  - d) Joseph's house

Question #5

Who dreamed that he was a sheaf of wheat and other sheaves bowed down to him?
  - a) Judah
  - b) Joseph
  - c) Daniel
  - d) Moses

Question #6

Who saw a sheet full of creatures and was told to "rise and eat"?
  - a) John
  - b) Peter
  - c) Stephen
  - d) James

Question #7

Who was warned in a dream not to go back to Herod?
  - a) wise men
  - b) shepherds
  - c) Joseph
  - d) John the Baptist

Question #8

Who was told in a dream to take a wife,
even though she was expecting a child?
- a) Hosea
- b) Joseph
- c) Moses
- d) Jacob

Question #9

Who was disturbed because she had a dream
about Jesus?
- a) Mary Magdalene
- b) Martha
- c) Herodias
- d) Pilate's wife

Question #10

In Daniel's prophetic dream of kingdoms to come,
how many beasts did Daniel see?
- a) 2
- b) 3
- c) 4
- d) 7

Biblical Dreams

ANSWERS

1. b) ladder (Genesis 28:12)
2. a) cattle (Genesis 41:20)
3. c) Daniel (Daniel 2:24)
4. c) jail (Genesis 40:1–3)
5. b) Joseph (Genesis 37:5–7)
6. b) Peter (Acts 10:9–13)
7. a) wise men (Matthew 2:1, 12)
8. b) Joseph (Matthew 1:20)
9. d) Pilate's wife (Matthew 27:17–19)
10. c) 4 (Daniel 7:3)

Did you outsmart the Sunday schoolers?

Can You
Outsmart
a
Sunday
Schooler?

The Bible mentions many kings and queens who influenced the nation of Israel. Some were good and some were evil. What do you know about these other countries and their monarchs?

Question #1

Balak, who hired Balaam to curse the Israelites, was king of the:
- a) Moabites
- b) Amorites
- c) Hittites
- d) Edomites

Question #2

The queen who came to visit Solomon was from:
- a) Babylon
- b) Egypt
- c) Sheba
- d) Ethiopia

Question #3

King Hiram (or Huram), from whom Solomon got materials to build the temple, was king of:
- a) Tyre
- b) Sidon
- c) Tyre and Sidon
- d) Syria

Question #4

Melchizedek was a priest, but he was also king of:
- a) Jericho
- b) Zion
- c) Jerusalem
- d) Salem

Question #5

Herod's official title was:
- a) king
- b) prince
- c) tetrach
- d) governor

Question #6

The king of Babylon who took the southern kingdom of Judah captive was:
- a) Darius
- b) Nebuchadnezzar
- c) Cyrus
- d) Belshazzar

Question #7

The king of what country took the northern kingdom of Israel captive?
- a) Egypt
- b) Assyria
- c) Syria
- d) Samaria

Question #8

The name of the king who allowed the Israelites to return to Jerusalem from their captivity in Babylon was:

  a) Nebuchadnezzar
  b) Darius
  c) Cyrus
  d) Ezra

Question #9

The king who saw the handwriting on the wall was:

  a) Belshazzar
  b) Nebuchadnezzar
  c) Darius
  d) Cyrus

Question #10

The name of the queen who was queen before Esther was:

  a) Bathsheba
  b) Vashti
  c) Abigail
  d) Ahinoam

Foreign Kings and Queens

ANSWERS

1. a) Moabites (Numbers 22:1–6)

2. c) Sheba (2 Chronicles 9:1)

3. a) Tyre (2 Chronicles 2:3)

4. d) Salem (Genesis 14:18)

5. c) tetrarch (Luke 3:1)

6. b) Nebuchadnezzar (2 Chronicles 36:6)

7. b) Assyria (2 Kings 17:6)

8. c) Cyrus (Ezra 1:1–2)

9. a) Belshazzar (Daniel 5:1–5)

10. b) Vashti (Esther 1:9)

Did you outsmart
the Sunday schoolers?

Can You
Outsmart
a
Sunday
Schooler?

Jesus called specific men to be his closest circle of followers and friends. He trusted these men to carry on His message after He had to leave them. He taught them many things. Can you identify them?

Question #1

Which three disciples were on the Mount of Transfiguration with Jesus?

    a) Peter, James, John
    b) Peter, Andrew, John
    c) Andrew, James, John
    d) James, Andrew, Peter

Question #2

When Jesus asked, "Who do you say that I am?" which disciple answered, "You are the Christ"?

    a) John   c) Philip
    b) Andrew   d) Peter

Question #3

Which disciple brought his brother to Jesus?

    a) James
    b) John
    c) Bartholomew
    d) Andrew

Question #4

Which disciple was a tax collector before he followed Jesus?

    a) Nathanael
    b) Matthew
    c) Judas
    d) Simon

Question #5

Which of the following was *not* a fisherman when Jesus called him?

    a) Peter
    b) Andrew
    c) James
    d) Nathanael

Question #6

Which disciple had *Iscariot* as part of his name?

    a) Simon
    b) Bartholomew
    c) Matthew
    d) Judas

Question #7

Which disciple demanded proof that Jesus had risen?

    a) Matthew   c) James
    b) Thomas   d) Peter

Question #8

Who cut off a man's ear?
- a) Judas
- b) Thomas
- c) Peter
- d) James

Question #9

Which disciple had Jesus heal his mother-in-law?
- a) John
- b) James
- c) Andrew
- d) Peter

Question #10

How many disciples were at the cross when Jesus was crucified?
- a) 11
- b) 7
- c) 3
- d) 1

Jesus' Disciples

ANSWERS

1. a) Peter, James, John
   (Matthew 17:1–2)

2. d) Peter (Matthew 16:15–16 NKJV)

3. d) Andrew (John 1:40–41)

4. b) Matthew (Matthew 9:9)

5. d) Nathanael (Matthew 4:18–22;
   John 1:45–48)

6. d) Judas (Mark 3:19)

7. b) Thomas (John 20:24–25)

8. c) Peter (John 18:10)

9. d) Peter (Matthew 8:14–15)

10. d) 1 (John 19:26)

Did you outsmart
the Sunday schoolers?

Can You
Outsmart
a
Sunday
Schooler?

The night before the battle of Jericho, Joshua asked the captain of the Lord's host, "Are You for us or for our adversaries?" (Joshua 5:13 NKJV). That's the question God asks His people: "Are you for Me or for My adversaries?" Who is on the Lord's side? The warriors in this quiz were. Do you know them?

Question #1

To which of His warriors did God say, "Have not I commanded thee? Be strong and of a good courage"?

  a) Moses
  b) David
  c) Joshua
  d) Jacob

Question #2

What woman nailed the enemy general's head to the ground?

  a) Jael
  b) Deborah
  c) Esther
  d) Miriam

Question #3

What Jewish leader had to rebuild the wall of Jerusalem with a sword in one hand?

a) David
b) Solomon
c) Nehemiah
d) Hezekiah

Question #4

The army that fought with pitchers and lamps shouted, "The sword of the LORD, and of _____."

a) Saul
b) Gideon
c) David
d) Joshua

Question #5

Saul's son who was David's friend was:

a) Abner
b) Joab
c) Absalom
d) Jonathan

Question #6

Which of God's prophets called down fire on two separate cohorts of fifty men each who had been sent to capture him?

a) Elijah
b) Elisha
c) Jeremiah
d) Isaiah

Question #7

Which judge of Israel who led the battle against the Ammonites was described as "a mighty man of valour"?

- a) Abimelech
- b) Jephthah
- c) Tola
- d) Jair

Question #8

Because Moses claimed he was slow of speech, whom did God send with him to confront Pharaoh?

- a) Joshua
- b) Caleb
- c) Aaron
- d) Amram

Question #9

Who was told, "Who knoweth whether thou art come to the kingdom for such a time as this?"—meaning that she might save her people.

- a) Deborah
- b) Miriam
- c) Esther
- d) Ruth

Question #10

Whom did God appoint to wipe out Ahab, Jezebel, and their evil offspring?

- a) Elijah
- b) Elisha
- c) Jehu
- d) Isaiah

God's Warriors

ANSWERS

1. c) Joshua (Joshua 1:9)

2. a) Jael (Judges 4:21)

3. c) Nehemiah (Nehemiah 4:18)

4. b) Gideon (Judges 7:18)

5. d) Jonathan (1 Samuel 19:2)

6. a) Elijah (2 Kings 1:10–14)

7. b) Jephthah (Judges 11:1)

8. c) Aaron (Exodus 4:10–16)

9. c) Esther (Esther 4:13–14)

10. c) Jehu (2 Kings 9:1–8)

Did you outsmart the Sunday schoolers?

Can You Outsmart a Sunday Schooler?

Animals played many important roles with people in the Bible. There were groups of clean and unclean animals. How many of the following animals are you familiar with?

Question #1

Jesus told His disciples to ask a man for a:
- a) donkey and colt
- b) camel
- c) sheep
- d) goat

Question #2

When Isaiah describes the righteous rule of God's anointed, he says that the lamb will dwell with the:
- a) lion
- b) wolf
- c) bear
- d) leopard

Question #3

When some young people mocked Elisha by calling him "bald head," what did God send to punish them?
- a) lions
- c) wolves
- b) bears
- d) both a and c

Question #4

Once every three years Solomon received tribute from Tarshish that included:

a) apes
b) peacocks
c) sheep
d) both a and b

Question #5

How many days and nights was Jonah in the belly of the great fish?

a) 1
b) 2
c) 3
d) 4

Question #6

Jesus said it was easier for a _____ to go through the eye of a needle than for a rich man to enter the kingdom of heaven.

a) camel
b) whale
c) leviathan
d) mouse

Question #7

God told Noah to take two of every animal—male and female—into the ark to keep them alive. How many of each *clean* animal was he to take?

a) 2
b) 3
c) 5
d) 7

Question #8

Abdon was a judge of Israel about whom little is recorded. However, the Bible does mention that he had seventy:

- a) colts
- b) cattle
- c) sheep
- d) camels

Question #9

When David told King Saul that he was willing to fight Goliath, he said that he had already killed:

- a) a lion and a bear
- b) a wolf and a bear
- c) a lion and a wolf
- d) a lion, a bear, and a wolf

Question #10

When Jesus cast devils out of the man who lived in the tombs, the devils asked Jesus to let them go into a nearby herd of:

- a) cattle
- b) sheep
- c) swine
- d) goats

Animals

ANSWERS

1. a) donkey and colt (Matthew 21:2)
2. b) wolf (Isaiah 11:1–6)
3. b) bears (2 Kings 2:23–24)
4. d) both a and b (1 Kings 10:22–23)
5. c) 3 (Jonah 1:17)
6. a) camel (Matthew 19:24)
7. d) 7 (Genesis 7:2)
8. a) colts (Judges 12:14)
9. a) a lion and a bear (1 Samuel 17:36)
10. c) swine (Mark 5:12)

Did you outsmart the Sunday schoolers?

Can You
Outsmart
a
Sunday
Schooler?

Hebrews 1:1 says that in the old days God spoke in diverse ways to the fathers by the prophets. The prophets prophesied good things and bad things and all things that God told them to. Sometimes they were listened to; sometimes they were persecuted. Do you know these prophets?

Question #1

What prophet did God hide by the brook Cherith and command ravens to feed him?

- a) Isaiah
- b) Jeremiah
- c) Elijah
- d) Elisha

Question #2

What was the test to see if a prophet was speaking God's word or not?

- a) his face would shine
- b) his words would be eloquent
- c) what he said would come to pass
- d) all of the above

Question #3

Deuteronomy 18:17–18 says that a prophet will be raised up like:

- a) Abraham
- b) Moses
- c) Joseph
- d) Elijah

Question #4

What Old Testament prophet saw the Lord sitting upon a throne?

    a) Elijah
    b) Elisha
    c) Isaiah
    d) Daniel

Question #5

What prophet was taken to heaven in a whirlwind and a chariot of fire?

    a) Moses
    b) Isaiah
    c) Elijah
    d) Elisha

Question #6

Who was known as the runaway prophet?

    a) Jeremiah
    b) Joel
    c) Jonah
    d) Jehu

Question #7

What two prophets appeared to Jesus on the Mount of Transfiguration?

    a) Elijah and Elisha
    b) Isaiah and Jeremiah
    c) Moses and Elisha
    d) Moses and Elijah

Question #8

What king had a proverb written about him that
said, "Is _____ also among the prophets?"

    a) Saul
    b) David
    c) Solomon
    d) Hezekiah

Question #9

What two prophets who also wrote books of the
Bible are mentioned in the book of Ezra?

    a) Haggai and Zechariah
    b) Habakkuk and Zephaniah
    c) Micah and Amos
    d) Isaiah and Jeremiah

Question #10

To whom did God say that He had ordained him to
be a prophet before he was born?

    a) Isaiah
    b) Micah
    c) Amos
    d) Jeremiah

Prophets

ANSWERS

1. c) Elijah (1 Kings 17:1–4)

2. c) what he said would come to pass (Deuteronomy 18:22)

3. b) Moses

4. c) Isaiah (Isaiah 6:1)

5. c) Elijah (2 Kings 2:11)

6. c) Jonah (Jonah 1:3)

7. d) Moses and Elijah (or Elias) (Matthew 17:3)

8. a) Saul (1 Samuel 10:12)

9. a) Haggai and Zechariah (Ezra 5:1)

10. d) Jeremiah (Jeremiah 1:5)

Did you outsmart the Sunday schoolers?

Can You Outsmart a Sunday Schooler?

The Bible is the Word of God. How much do you know about its physical properties? Who wrote it? How long is it? With which of the following facts are you familiar?

Question #1

How many chapters are in the Song of Solomon?

- a) 4
- b) 6
- c) 8
- d) 10

Question #2

What book of the New Testament is totally dedicated to describing God's love for us?

- a) 1 John
- b) 2 Peter
- c) Romans
- d) 1 Corinthians

Question #3

What is the longest chapter in the Bible?

- a) Psalm 19
- b) Psalm 119
- c) Revelation 20
- d) 1 Corinthians 15

Question #4

What two books of the Bible mention the tree of life?

    a)   Genesis and Psalms
    b)   Genesis and Proverbs
    c)   Genesis and Revelation
    d)   Genesis and Matthew

Question #5

How many books are in the Old Testament?

    a)   27
    b)   29
    c)   37
    d)   39

Question #6

How many books are in the New Testament?

    a)   27
    b)   29
    c)   37
    d)   39

Question #7

What is the last book of the Old Testament?

    a)   Haggai
    b)   Zephaniah
    c)   Zechariah
    d)   Malachi

Question #8

The first five books of the Bible are commonly referred to as the books of:
   a) law
   b) history
   c) poetry
   d) prophecy

Question #9

How many books of the Bible start with the letter *J*?
   a) 8
   b) 10
   c) 12
   d) 14

Question #10

How many books of the Bible have only one chapter?
   a) 2
   b) 3
   c) 4
   d) 5

The B-I-B-L-E

ANSWERS

1. c) 8

2. a) 1 John

3. b) Psalm 119

4. c) Genesis and Revelation (Genesis 3:22; Revelation 2:7)

5. d) 39

6. a) 27

7. d) Malachi

8. a) law

9. c) 12 (Joshua, Judges, Job, Jeremiah, Joel, Jonah, John, James, 1 John, 2 John, 3 John, Jude)

10. d) 5 (Obadiah, Philemon, 2 John, 3 John, Jude)

Did you outsmart the Sunday schoolers?

Can You
Outsmart
a
Sunday
Schooler?

Many times when God spoke to His people, He asked them questions. Sometimes He spoke to them directly and sometimes He spoke to them through a prophet or an angel. Do you know to whom God was speaking when He asked the following questions?

Question #1

"Why are you angry?"
- a) Elijah
- b) Abraham
- c) Cain
- d) Adam

Question #2

"What is that in your hand?"
- a) David
- b) Moses
- c) Saul
- d) Jacob

Question #3

"Ask! What shall I give you?"
- a) Solomon
- b) David
- c) Abraham
- d) Isaac

Question #4

"From where do you come?"
- a) Paul
- b) Satan
- c) Esau
- d) Noah

Question #5

"Where were you when I laid the foundations of the earth?"
- a) Adam
- b) Noah
- c) Job
- d) Elijah

Question #6

"Whom shall I send, and who will go for us?"
- a) Isaiah
- b) Ezekiel
- c) Daniel
- d) Jeremiah

Question #7

"Is it right for you to be angry?"
- a) Job
- b) Jeremiah
- c) Jonah
- d) James

Question #8

"Is anything too hard for the LORD?"
   a) Abraham
   b) Isaac
   c) Jacob
   d) Joseph

Question #9

"What have I done to you? And how have I wearied you?"
   a) Solomon
   b) Jeremiah
   c) the nation of Israel
   d) Pharaoh

Question #10

"Where are you?"
   a) Adam
   b) Eve
   c) Adam and Eve
   d) the serpent

God's Questions

ANSWERS

1. c) Cain (Genesis 4:6 NKJV)

2. b) Moses (Exodus 4:2 NKJV)

3. a) Solomon (1 Kings 3:5 NKJV)

4. b) Satan (Job 1:7 NKJV)

5. c) Job (Job 38:4 NKJV)

6. a) Isaiah (Isaiah 6:8)

7. c) Jonah (Jonah 4:4 NKJV)

8. a) Abraham (Genesis 18:14 NKJV)

9. c) the nation of Israel (Micah 6:3 NKJV)

10. a) Adam (Genesis 3:9 NKJV)

Did you outsmart
the Sunday schoolers?

Can You Outsmart a Sunday Schooler?

The book of Judges shows how the Israelites followed a destructive cycle. Things would be going well, and the Israelites would start following other gods. Then they would be oppressed by some enemy and cry out to the Lord. The Lord would raise up a judge to deliver them. After they were delivered, the Israelites would remain faithful to the Lord as long as the judge lived. When the judge died, the Israelites would once again start worshipping other gods. The book of Judges shows the faithfulness of God to deliver His people. What do you know about these judges?

Question #1

What judge turned down the opportunity to be king when the people of Israel offered him that position?

a) Abdon   c) Gideon
b) Tola   d) Jair

Question #2

Who was the judge set apart to God by a Nazarite vow?

a) Othniel
b) Samson
c) Jepthah
d) Gideon

Question #3

How was the judge Othniel related to Caleb?
He was his:

    a) nephew
    b) brother
    c) son-in-law
    d) both a and c

Question #4

One judge had to fight against the king of Moab
named Eglon, who was described as:

    a) a mighty warrior
    b) a fierce warrior
    c) a very fat man
    d) an evil king

Question #5

Who was called the left-handed judge?

    a) Tola   c) Ehud
    b) Jair   d) Othniel

Question #6

Samson lost his strength when Delilah:

    a) tied him to the bed
    b) bound him with new ropes
    c) wove his hair into a loom
    d) cut his hair

Question #7

The only female judge, Deborah, helped Barak fight against the general named:

  a) Hazael
  b) Jehu
  c) Sisera
  d) Anak

Question #8

The enemies whom Samson fought were the:

  a) Moabites
  b) Ammonites
  c) Canaanites
  d) Philistines

Question #9

Jephthah vowed to sacrifice the first thing that came out of his house if he won the battle against the Ammonites. What came out of his house?

  a) a cow
  b) a sheep
  c) a dog
  d) his daughter

Question #10

Deborah dwelt under what kind of tree?

  a) sycamore   c) palm
  b) fig   d) tamarisk

Judges

ANSWERS

1. c) Gideon (Judges 8:22–23)
2. b) Samson (Judges 13:5, 24)
3. d) both a and c (Judges 1:13)
4. c) a very fat man (Judges 3:17)
5. c) Ehud (Judges 3:15)
6. d) cut his hair (Judges 16:19–20)
7. c) Sisera (Judges 4:13–14)
8. d) Philistines (Judges 16:30)
9. d) his daughter (Judges 11:30–34)
10. c) palm (Judges 4:4–5)

Did you outsmart the Sunday schoolers?

Can You
Outsmart
a
Sunday
Schooler?

Unlike the kings of Israel, who were all evil, there were some really good kings of Judah, as well as some evil ones. The kings of Judah were all descended from David, and it was from this kingly line that Jesus came. Which of these kings do you know?

Question #1

What king's grandmother tried to kill all of her grandchildren so she could be queen?

    a) Joash
    b) Hezekiah
    c) Manasseh
    d) Josiah

Question #2

Like Ahab, which king built up a grove for the worship of false god?

    a) Asa
    b) Manasseh
    c) Jeconiah
    d) Jehoram

Question #3

How many times was David anointed king?

    a) 1   c) 3
    b) 2   d) 4

Question #4

What prophet, along with Zadok the priest, anointed Solomon king?

- a) Elijah
- b) Elisha
- c) Isaiah
- d) Nathan

Question #5

Who was the king when the kingdom split into the northern ten tribes (Israel) and the southern two tribes (Judah)?

- a) Solomon
- b) Rehoboam
- c) Hezekiah
- d) David

Question #6

About what boy king does the Bible say there was none before him or after him "that turned to the LORD with all his heart"?

- a) Joash
- b) Jehoram
- c) Jehu
- d) Josiah

Question #7

Uzziah was one of the really good kings of Judah, but God struck him with leprosy because he:

    a) accidentally killed someone
    b) took God's name in vain
    c) burned incense in the temple
    d) b and c

Question #8

What king had a brother named Adonijah who tried to steal his throne?

    a) David
    b) Solomon
    c) Asa
    d) Jotham

Question #9

Who was king when the kingdom of Judah was taken into Babylonian captivity?

    a) Hezekiah
    b) Manasseh
    c) Jehoiakim
    d) Hazael

Question #10

Who was the first king of Judah?

    a) Saul   c) Solomon
    b) David   d) Rehoboam

Kings of Judah

ANSWERS

1. a) Joash (2 Chronicles 22:10–11)

2. b) Manasseh (2 Kings 21:1–3)

3. c) 3 (1 Samuel 16:13; 2 Samuel 2:4; 5:3)

4. d) Nathan (1 Kings 1:34)

5. b) Rehoboam (1 Kings 12:19–21)

6. d) Josiah (2 Kings 23:24–25)

7. c) burned incense in the temple (2 Chronicles 26:19–20)

8. b) Solomon (1 Kings 1:5, 17–18)

9. c) Jehoiakim (2 Chronicles 36:5–6)

10. a) Saul (1 Samuel 10:21–24)

Did you outsmart the Sunday schoolers?

Can You Outsmart a Sunday Schooler?

After the kingdom split into Israel and Judah, there was not one king of Israel whom the Bible refers to as good. Nor was there a royal succession. The kings of Israel usually became king by killing a predecessor. What do you know about these bad boys?

Question #1

What was the shortest reign of a king of Israel?

    a) 1 day   c) 5 days
    b) 3 days   d) 7 days

Question #2

After the kingdom split into the ten northern tribes (Israel) and the two southern tribes (Judah), who was the first king of the northern tribes?

    a) Jehu   c) Jeroboam
    b) Ahab   d) Jotham

Question #3

About which king does the Bible say that he did more evil in the sight of the Lord than all who were before him?

    a) Ahab   c) Omni
    b) Zimri   d) Jehu

Question #4

What king was described as "higher than any of the people from his shoulders and upward"?

    a) Saul
    b) Jehu
    c) Jehoshaphat
    d) Ben-hadad

Question #5

After the kingdom split, how many kings did the ten northern tribes have before they were taken into captivity?

    a) 20   c) 30
    b) 25   d) 35

Question #6

What nation took the ten northern tribes into captivity?

    a) Assyria
    b) Syria
    c) Babylon
    d) Egypt

Question #7

Who was king when the ten northern tribes were taken into captivity?

    a) Ahab   c) Hoshea
    b) Zimri   d) Omni

Question #8

Whom did Jezebel have stoned to death so Ahab
could steal his vineyard?
- a) Nehemiah
- b) Nabal
- c) Naboth
- d) Nathan

Question #9

After the kingdom split, what was the longest
period of time that a king reigned over Israel?
- a) 30 years
- b) 31 years
- c) 40 years
- d) 41 years

Question #10

What son of a king of Judah married the daughter
of a king of Israel?
- a) Rehoboam
- b) Hezekiah
- c) Jehoram
- d) Manasseh

Kings of Israel

ANSWERS

1. d) 7 days (1 Kings 16:15)
2. c) Jeroboam (1 Kings 11:31)
3. a) Ahab (1 Kings 16:30)
4. a) Saul (1 Samuel 10:21, 23)
5. a) 20
6. a) Assyria (2 Kings 17:6)
7. c) Hoshea (2 Kings 17:6)
8. c) Naboth (1 Kings 21:8–11)
9. d) 41 years (2 Kings 14:23)
10. c) Jehoram (2 Chronicles 21:1, 6)

Did you outsmart
the Sunday schoolers?

Can You
Outsmart
a
Sunday
Schooler?

All through the Old Testament, God's people turned from worshipping Him and instead worshipped false gods and idols. It broke God's heart and caused all kinds of troubles for the Israelites. Some of the false gods are more well-known to us than others. How many have you heard of?

Question #1

A king of Israel put what kind of idols in the cities of Dan and Bethel?

- a) idols to Baal
- b) idols to Ashteroth
- c) stone pillars
- d) golden calves

Question #2

What princess of Sidon (or Zidon) introduced Baal worship to Israel?

- a) Bathsheba
- b) Athaliah
- c) Jezebel
- d) Abigail

Question #3

Hezekiah destroyed what popular idol?
- a) the brass snake Moses made in the wilderness
- b) the golden calf Aaron made
- c) Baal
- d) Ashteroth

Question #4

What idol of the Philistines fell facedown in front of the ark of the covenant?
- a) Molech
- b) Chemosh
- c) Beelzebub
- d) Dagon

Question #5

Into what did King Josiah transform the places of idolatry?
- a) cemeteries
- b) meadows
- c) wastelands
- d) potters' fields

Question #6

The only mention of an idol in the New Testament is the goddess Diana, whose shrine was in what city?
- a) Philippi
- b) Macedonia
- c) Ephesus
- d) Colosse

Question #7

What were men building when God confused their speech and language?

a) an altar   c) a castle
b) a tower   d) a temple

Question #8

What king of Israel was the first to build places for the worship of Chemosh and Molech?

a) Ahab   c) Solomon
b) Jehu   d) Zimri

Question #9

What judge of Israel pulled down his own father's altar to Baal because God commanded him to?

a) Samson
b) Othniel
c) Gideon
d) Jephthah

Question #10

What king had Daniel thrown in the lions' den because Daniel refused to pray to him instead of praying to God?

a) Nebuchadnezzar
b) Darius
c) Cyrus
d) Belshazzar

False Gods

ANSWERS

1. d) golden calves (1 Kings 12:28–29)

2. c) Jezebel (1 Kings 16:31–32)

3. a) the brass snake Moses made in the wilderness (2 Kings 18:1, 4)

4. d) Dagon (1 Samuel 5:1–3)

5. a) cemeteries (2 Kings 23:13–14)

6. c) Ephesus (Acts 19:24–28)

7. b) a tower (Genesis 11:4–9)

8. c) Solomon (1 Kings 11:7)

9. c) Gideon (Judges 6:24–25)

10. b) Darius (Daniel 6:9–16)

Did you outsmart the Sunday schoolers?

Can You Outsmart a Sunday Schooler?

All through the Bible there are stories of people who wanted their own way and would do anything to get it. They didn't care about God's will, just their own. These people are a warning to us about how *not* to behave. How well do you know their stories?

Question #1

Who said to God, "My punishment is greater than I can bear"?

a) Ahab
b) Jezebel
c) Cain
d) Saul

Question #2

Which queen "destroyed all the seed royal of the house of Judah" and took the throne for herself?

a) Bathsheba
b) Athaliah
c) Vashti
d) Jezebel

Question #3

Nadab and Abihu, who were burned up because they offered strange fire to the Lord, were the sons of what high priest?

a) Aaron
b) Caiaphas
c) Eli
d) Melchizedek

Question #4

Herod was an Idumean, a descendant of the Edomites, whose forefather was:

a) Ishmael
b) Cain
c) Lot
d) Esau

Question #5

After Jacob worked seven years to earn the right to marry Rachel, who tricked him and gave him Leah instead?

a) Betheuel
b) Haran
c) Laban
d) Lot

Question #6

Haman was so determined to kill Mordecai that he:

a) tried to kill all the Jews
b) built a gallows to hang Mordecai on
c) tried to stab Mordecai
d) both a and b

Question #7

The group that Jesus pronounced woes upon was the:

a) Sadducees
b) scribes and Pharisees
c) priests
d) Zealots

Question #8

Whom did Pharaoh tell to kill all the Hebrew baby boys?

- a) midwives
- b) soldiers
- c) the babies' parents
- d) his chief servant

Question #9

Absalom, David's son who led a rebellion against his father, was finally captured and killed because:

- a) his hair got caught in a tree
- b) his servants turned on him
- c) the Lord struck him down
- d) his own soldiers captured him

Question #10

Who ordered John the Baptist's head to be cut off?

- a) Herodias
- b) Herod
- c) Salome
- d) Pilate

Bad Guys and Gals

ANSWERS

1. c) Cain (Genesis 4:13)

2. b) Athaliah (2 Chronicles 22:10, 12)

3. a) Aaron (Leviticus 10:1–2)

4. d) Esau (Genesis 36:1)

5. c) Laban (Genesis 29:21–25)

6. d) both a and b (Esther 3:5–6; 5:14)

7. b) scribes and Pharisees
        (Matthew 23:15)

8. a) midwives (Exodus 1:15–16)

9. a) his hair got caught in a tree
        (2 Samuel 14:25–26; 18:9)

10. b) Herod (Matthew 14:6–10)

Did you outsmart
the Sunday schoolers?

Can You
Outsmart
a
Sunday
Schooler?

The Promised Land

Even today the phrase "the Promised Land" is very common. People use it to describe desirable places they would like to go. In the Bible the Promised Land was a very specific place that God gave to His people. How much do you know about the Promised Land?

Question #1

To whom was the Promised Land originally promised?

a) Abraham
b) Isaac
c) Jacob
d) Moses

Question #2

When the twelve spies returned from the Promised Land, what did they carry on a pole between two men?

a) a basket of apples
b) a cluster of grapes
c) a small olive tree
d) a huge honeycomb

Question #3

What excuse did the spies give for not wanting to go into the Promised Land?

a) the cities were walled and fortified
b) the land ate up its inhabitants
c) the people were giants
d) all of the above

Question #4

Who led the people into the Promised Land?
- a) Moses
- b) Joshua
- c) Caleb
- d) God—in His pillar of cloud

Question #5

Whose bones were carried from Egypt to be buried in the Promised Land?
- a) Abraham
- b) Isaac
- c) Jacob
- d) Joseph

Question #6

How many spies returned with a good report?
- a) 2
- b) 6
- c) 10
- d) 12

Question #7

What body of water did God part so that the people could enter into the Promised Land?
- a) the Red Sea
- b) the Dead Sea
- c) the Jordan River
- d) the Sea of Galilee

Question #8

What group of people tricked Joshua into not fighting them by pretending they were from far away?

- a) the Jebusites
- b) the Gibeonites
- c) the Hittites
- d) the Hivites

Question #9

Achan's sin put all of the Israelites at risk when they went to fight Ai. His sin was that he:

- a) stole treasure from Jericho
- b) blasphemed God
- c) refused to fight
- d) committed adultery

Question #10

As a result of his sin, Achan and his family were:

- a) stoned
- b) burned with fire
- c) banished from the Promised Land
- d) both a and b

The Promised Land

ANSWERS

1. a) Abraham (Genesis 13:14–17; 17:5)
2. b) a cluster of grapes (Numbers 13:23)
3. d) all of the above (Numbers 13:28, 32–33)
4. b) Joshua (Joshua 1:1–2)
5. d) Joseph (Exodus 13:19)
6. a) 2 (Numbers 14:6–7)
7. c) the Jordan River (Joshua 3:15–16)
8. b) the Gibeonites (Joshua 9:3–9)
9. a) stole treasure from Jericho (Joshua 6:2, 18; 7:1–11)
10. d) both a and b (Joshua 7:25)

Did you outsmart the Sunday schoolers?

Can You

Outsmart

a

Sunday

Schooler?

Our God is a God of awesome might and power. Throughout the Bible He shows Himself as compassionate as well as powerful. God used miracles to help as well as awe His people. What do you know about these miracles?

Question #1

What prophet's bones revived a dead man?
- a) Elijah
- b) Elisha
- c) Isaiah
- d) Jeremiah

Question #2

Which of the following miracles was performed by both Elijah and Elisha?
- a) making an ax head float
- b) making bitter water drinkable
- c) parting the waters of the Jordan River
- d) calling fire down from heaven

Question #3

How many times did Naaman have to dip himself in the Jordan River to get his leprosy cured?
- a) 1
- b) 3
- c) 7
- d) 10

Question #4

What prophet told a king there would be no rain until the prophet said so?

a) Jeremiah
b) Daniel
c) Nathan
d) Elijah

Question #5

Who was Joshua fighting against when God made the sun stand still?

a) the Moabites
b) the Amorites
c) the Edomites
d) the Philistines

Question #6

What king of Judah saw a sundial go back ten degrees as a sign from God?

a) Solomon
b) Joash
c) Hezekiah
d) Jehoshaphat

Question #7

What was Moses doing when he saw the burning bush?

a) drawing water from a well
b) digging a well
c) tending sheep
d) nothing

Question #8

When Dorcas, who did many good works, died, which apostle raised her from the dead?
- a) Paul
- b) Peter
- c) James
- d) John

Question #9

What miracle was performed by both Paul and Peter?
- a) making someone go blind
- b) casting out demons
- c) curing a lame man
- d) both b and c

Question #10

What did God tell Moses to stretch out over the sea so that the waters would part?
- a) his hand
- b) his rod
- c) the ark of the covenant
- d) both a and b

Biblical Miracles

ANSWERS

1. b) Elisha (2 Kings 13:21)

2. c) parting the waters of the Jordan River (2 Kings 2:8, 14)

3. c) 7 (2 Kings 5:14)

4. d) Elijah (1 Kings 17:1)

5. b) the Amorites (Joshua 10:12–13)

6. c) Hezekiah (Isaiah 38:4–8)

7. c) tending sheep (Exodus 3:1–2)

8. b) Peter (Acts 9:39–40)

9. c) curing a lame man (Acts 3:4–8; 14:8–10)

10. d) both a and b (Exodus 14:16)

Did you outsmart the Sunday schoolers?

Can You
Outsmart
a
Sunday
Schooler?

The Garden of Eden was truly paradise on earth. God created this perfect garden so that humankind would have a place to live and grow and learn about God. How much have you learned about the Garden of Eden and what happened there?

Question #1

How many rivers were in Eden?

a) 1 c) 3
b) 2 d) 4

Question #2

God made Eve from:

a) dust
b) clay
c) Adam's rib
d) stone

Question #3

In what area of the garden was the tree of life located?

a) east
b) west
c) middle
d) south

Question #4

Which tree did the Lord command Adam not to eat from?

- a) the tree of life
- b) the tree of wisdom
- c) the tree of evil
- d) the tree of the knowledge of good and evil

Question #5

What did God say would happen if Adam ate from the forbidden tree?

- a) he would be banished
- b) he would become sick
- c) he would die
- d) he would lose Eve

Question #6

What were Eve and the serpent talking about when she was tempted?

- a) a river
- b) a meadow
- c) a field
- d) a tree

Question #7

What did the serpent tell Eve would happen if she ate from the forbidden tree?

- a) you will not die
- b) you will become as gods
- c) you will know good and evil
- d) all of the above

Question #8

After they ate from the forbidden tree, what was Adam and Eve's first reaction?

    a)   they got sick
    b)   they hid themselves
    c)   they clothed themselves
    d)   they ran away from the serpent

Question #9

As a result of Adam's sin, God cursed:

    a)   Adam
    b)   the serpent
    c)   the ground
    d)   both b and c

Question #10

God banished Adam and Eve from the garden to prevent them from:

    a)   hiding from Him
    b)   killing the serpent
    c)   living forever
    d)   destroying the forbidden tree

The Garden of Eden

ANSWERS

1. a) 1 (Genesis 2:10)
2. c) Adam's rib (Genesis 2:21–22; 3:20)
3. c) middle (Genesis 2:9)
4. d) the tree of the knowledge of good and evil (Genesis 2:16–17)
5. c) he would die (Genesis 2:16–17)
6. d) a tree (Genesis 3:1–6)
7. d) all of the above (Genesis 3:4–5)
8. c) they clothed themselves (Genesis 3:7)
9. d) both b and c (Genesis 3:14, 17)
10. c) living forever (Genesis 3:22)

Did you outsmart the Sunday schoolers?

Can You
Outsmart
a
Sunday
Schooler?

Sometimes we may quote a verse that is very familiar to us, but perhaps we're not so certain where to find it in the Bible. Following are ten well-known verses. Do you know their correct biblical references?

Question #1

"Jesus wept."

- a) Matthew 11:35
- b) Mark 11:35
- c) John 11:35
- d) Luke 11:35

Question #2

"Am I my brother's keeper?"

- a) Genesis 2:9
- b) Genesis 3:9
- c) Genesis 4:9
- d) Genesis 5:9

Question #3

"Father, forgive them; for they know not what they do."

- a) Luke 23:34
- b) Matthew 23:34
- c) John 19:34
- d) Mark 14:34

Question #4

"The LORD is my shepherd; I shall not want."

a) Psalm 1:1
b) Psalm 100:1
c) Psalm 23:1
d) Psalm 19:1

Question #5

"For God so loved the world, that he gave his only begotten Son, that whosoever believeth in him should not perish, but have everlasting life."

a) John 1:16
b) John 2:16
c) John 3:16
d) John 4:16

Question #6

"Make a joyful noise unto the LORD, all ye lands."

a) Psalm 1:1
b) Psalm 34:1
c) Psalm 90:1
d) Psalm 100:1

Question #7

"With God all things are possible."

a) Matthew 19:26
b) Matthew 9:26
c) Matthew 11:26
d) Matthew 13:26

Question #8

"Not my will, but thine, be done."
   a) Luke 22:42
   b) Matthew 26:39
   c) Mark 14:36
   d) all of the above

Question #9

"Pride goeth before destruction, and an haughty spirit before a fall."
   a) Proverbs 3:5
   b) Proverbs 16:18
   c) Proverbs 1:7
   d) Proverbs 31:1

Question #10

"Train up a child in the way he should go: and when he is old, he will not depart from it."
   a) Proverbs 22:6
   b) Ecclesiastes 3:3
   c) Psalm 22:6
   d) Proverbs 18:24

Where Is This Verse Found?

ANSWERS

1. c) John 11:35
2. c) Genesis 4:9
3. a) Luke 23:34
4. c) Psalm 23:1
5. c) John 3:16
6. d) Psalm 100:1
7. a) Matthew 19:26
8. a) Luke 22:42
9. b) Proverbs 16:18
10. a) Proverbs 22:6

Did you outsmart the Sunday schoolers?

Can You
Outsmart
a
Sunday
Schooler?

The Israelites were proud of their heritage, and they kept lengthy records of their lineage in order to prove who they were and from whom they were descended. In addition to the following quiz, here is one more question: Can you name the twelve tribes of Israel?

Question #1

The tribes were named for the twelve sons of:

    a) Joseph
    b) Jacob
    c) Moses
    d) Isaac

Question #2

There are three Sauls mentioned in the Bible, two of major importance—King Saul and the man who became the apostle Paul. They were both from the tribe of:

    a) Levi
    b) Ephraim
    c) Judah
    d) Benjamin

Question #3

The tribe of Joseph became the two tribes of:
- a) Manasseh and Ephraim
- b) Gad and Dan
- c) Manasseh and Naphtali
- d) Ephraim and Dan

Question #4

From what tribe was John the Baptist?
- a) Judah
- b) Reuben
- c) Levi
- d) Benjamin

Question #5

What tribe moved from their allotted inheritance in the Promised Land because they couldn't defeat the Canaanites on their land?
- a) Asher
- b) Reuben
- c) Dan
- d) Simeon

Question #6

Forty-two thousand men of Ephraim were slaughtered because they could not pronounce the word:
- a) *maranatha*
- b) *anathema*
- c) *shibboleth*
- d) *hosanna*

Question #7

When Israel entered the Promised Land, how many tribes stayed east of Jordan?

- a) 3
- b) 6
- c) 9
- d) 12

Question #8

When the kingdom of Israel split into the northern ten tribes and the southern two tribes, the two southern tribes were Judah and:

- a) Reuben
- b) Naphtali
- c) Benjamin
- d) Levi

Question #9

The only tribe whose name begins with *Z* is:

- a) Zechariah
- b) Zephaniah
- c) Zipporah
- d) Zebulun

Question #10

In the lists of the tribes of Israel, which tribe is almost always listed first?

- a) Judah
- b) Reuben
- c) Simeon
- d) Levi

Tribes of Israel

ANSWERS

1. b) Jacob (Exodus 1:1–6)

2. d) Benjamin (1 Samuel 9:1–2; Philippians 3:5)

3. a) Manasseh and Ephraim (Genesis 48:1–6)

4. c) Levi (Luke 1:5–13, 57–60)

5. c) Dan (Judges 18:1–10, 26–29)

6. c) *shibboleth* (Judges 12:5–6)

7. a) 3 (Numbers 32:33)

8. c) Benjamin (1 Kings 12:23)

9. d) Zebulun (Genesis 49:13)

10. b) Reuben (Genesis 49:3)

Did you outsmart the Sunday schoolers?

Can You
Outsmart
a
Sunday
Schooler?

The Bible says that God uses foolish things to confound the wise, and He uses weak things to confound the mighty. Nothing is too small for God to use to His glory. Of course, we have to be willing to let Him use us. What do you know about these little things God used?

Question #1

Because Rahab believed in God and hid the Israelite spies, God told her she would not perish in Jericho if she bound a _____ in her window.

- a) new rope
- b) loom
- c) bundle of straw
- d) scarlet thread

Question #2

How many stones did David take out of the brook when he went to fight Goliath?

- a) 3
- b) 4
- c) 5
- d) 6

Question #3

Shamgar was a judge of Israel who used what to slay six hundred Philistines?

- a) an ox goad
- b) the jawbone of an ass
- c) a sling
- d) a shepherd's staff

Question #4

To show that Aaron was His choice for high priest, God made Aaron's rod:

- a) longer
- b) shorter
- c) turn into a snake
- d) blossom

Question #5

Samson used what to slay a thousand of Israel's enemies?

- a) an ox goad
- b) the jawbone of an ass
- c) a sling
- d) a shepherd's staff

Question #6

When a prophet's widow needed money to save her sons, Elisha multiplied her last pot of:

- a) oil
- b) corn
- c) meal
- d) wheat

Question #7

When Jesus needed to pay the temple tax, He directed Peter to find a coin where?

- a) in a nearby field
- b) in the mouth of a fish
- c) in the middle of the road
- d) in a tree

Question #8

When the poor widow gave her two mites, she gave:

    a) what the temple required
    b) money that she had found
    c) all she had
    d) what the priest told her to give

Question #9

When Moses asked the people to bring offerings for the making of the tabernacle, they brought gold:

    a) bracelets
    b) earrings
    c) rings
    d) all of the above

Question #10

When Elisha succeeded Elijah, what did he receive of Elijah's as a symbol of his succession?

    a) a mantle
    b) a rod
    c) a ring
    d) a robe

God's Little Things

ANSWERS

1. d) scarlet thread (Joshua 2:18)

2. c) 5 (1 Samuel 17:40)

3. a) an ox goad (Judges 3:31)

4. d) blossom (Numbers 17:1–8)

5. b) the jawbone of an ass (Judges 15:16)

6. a) oil (2 Kings 4:1–7)

7. b) in the mouth of a fish (Matthew 17:24–27)

8. c) all she had (Mark 12:42–44)

9. d) all of the above (Exodus 35:5, 21–22)

10. a) a mantle (2 Kings 2:9–13)

Did you outsmart the Sunday schoolers?

Can You
Outsmart
a
Sunday
Schooler?

Psalm 19:7 says, "The law of the LORD is perfect, converting the soul." Many people talk about the Ten Commandments, but what do you really know about them and the circumstances surrounding the way they were given? Can you name each of the Ten Commandments?

Question #1

God wrote the first set of tablets with His finger. After Moses broke the original tablets, who wrote the second set?

- a) God
- b) Moses
- c) Aaron
- d) Joshua

Question #2

What two Old Testament books list the Ten Commandments?

- a) Exodus and Deuteronomy
- b) Exodus and Leviticus
- c) Leviticus and Deuteronomy
- d) Deuteronomy and Numbers

Question #3

When Moses came down from the mountain, he broke the first set of tablets because the Israelites were:

- a) worshipping a golden calf
- b) shouting
- c) dancing
- d) all of the above

Question #4

What is promised to those who honor their fathers and mothers?

- a) their own children will honor them
- b) others will honor them
- c) their days will be long in the land
- d) they will be prosperous

Question #5

"Remember the sabbath" is what number commandment?

- a) 3
- b) 4
- c) 5
- d) 6

Question #6

The last commandment in the list is, "Thou shalt not_____."

- a) kill
- b) steal
- c) commit adultery
- d) covet

Question #7

The first commandment is:
a) "Love the Lord with all your heart"
b) "Hear, O Israel, the Lord your God is one"
c) "Thou shalt have no other gods before me"
d) "Love your neighbor as yourself"

Question #8

How many days and nights was Moses up on the mountain to receive the Ten Commandments?
a) 7
b) 14
c) 30
d) 40

Question #9

Although Moses could go up on the mountain, God warned the rest of the people to stay away. If anyone came near the mountain, he would be:
a) struck by lightning
b) hanged
c) stoned
d) swallowed up by the earth

Question #10

But one man was allowed to go up on the mountain with Moses. That man was:
a) Aaron
b) Caleb
c) Joshua
d) Eleazar

The Ten Commandments

ANSWERS

1. b) Moses (Exodus 34:27–29)

2. a) Exodus and Deuteronomy (Exodus 20:1–17; Deuteronomy 5:6–21)

3. d) all of the above (Exodus 32:17–19)

4. c) their days will be long in the land (Exodus 20:12)

5. b) 4 (Exodus 20:8)

6. d) covet (Exodus 20:17)

7. c) "Thou shalt have no other gods before me" (Exodus 20:3)

8. d) 40 (Deuteronomy 9:9)

9. c) stoned (Exodus 19:12–13)

10. c) Joshua (Exodus 24:13–14)

Did you outsmart the Sunday schoolers?

Can You
Outsmart
a
Sunday
Schooler?

The Bible is full of families. Just like today's families, some are well-functioning and some are dysfunctional. All of them are there for us to learn from. Family lineage was extremely important in the Bible. It's interesting to see who was related to whom and how. What do you know about the following families?

Question #1

Mephibosheth was the son of:

a) David   c) Jonathan

b) Saul   d) Jesse

Question #2

David was Solomon's father. Who was Solomon's mother?

a) Michal

b) Abigail

c) Bathsheba

d) Abishag

Question #3

How was Methuselah related to Noah?

a) father

b) grandfather

c) great-grandfather

d) great-great-grandfather

Question #4

How were Ruth and Boaz related to David?
    a) grandparents
    b) aunt and uncle
    c) cousins
    d) great-grandparents

Question #5

How was Jesus related to John the Baptist?
    a) their mothers were cousins
    b) their fathers were cousins
    c) Jesus' mother and John's father
       were cousins
    d) Jesus' earthly father and John's mother
       were cousins

Question #6

Lot was Abraham's:
    a) nephew   c) uncle
    b) cousin   d) brother

Question #7

How was Seth related to Cain?
    a) son
    b) brother
    c) nephew
    d) uncle

Question #8

Jochebed was Moses':
    a) mother
    b) mother-in-law
    c) father
    d) father-in-law

Question #9

Jesus' disciples James and John were:
    a) cousins
    b) brothers
    c) father and son
    d) uncle and nephew

Question #10

Samuel's mother, who prayed to have a son and then dedicated him to God, was:
    a) Hannah
    b) Ruth
    c) Rachel
    d) Leah

Biblical Relatives

ANSWERS

1. c) Jonathan (2 Samuel 9:6)

2. c) Bathsheba (1 Kings 1:11)

3. b) grandfather (Genesis 5:25–29)

4. d) great-grandparents (Ruth 4:21–22)

5. a) their mothers were cousins
   (Luke 1:36, 60)

6. a) nephew (Genesis 11:31)

7. b) brother (Genesis 4:1; 5:3)

8. a) mother (Exodus 6:20)

9. b) brothers (Matthew 4:21)

10. a) Hannah (1 Samuel 1:9–11, 19–20)

Did you outsmart
the Sunday schoolers?

Can You
Outsmart
a
Sunday
Schooler?

"Wherefore let him that thinketh he standeth take heed lest he fall" (1 Corinthians 10:12). Sometimes it is when we feel strongest that we make mistakes. Mistakes can be a good learning tool if we only look at them in the right light. The following biblical situations have a lot to teach us. What do you already know about these mistakes?

Question #1

To whom was the prophet Nathan speaking when he pointed out this king's sin with the words, "Thou art the man"?

    a) Saul
    b) David
    c) Solomon
    d) Jeroboam

Question #2

The king who threw Daniel into the lions' den couldn't change the bad law that he had passed because:

    a) he didn't want to
    b) the people who tricked him into it wouldn't let him
    c) he thought it would make him look weak
    d) the law of his land said he couldn't

Question #3

Jesus told Peter that he would deny Him three times before the cock crowed how many times?

a) 1
b) 2

c) 3
d) 4

Question #4

Moses wasn't allowed to go into the Promised Land because:

a) he was too old
b) he didn't want to
c) he let the people turn away when they first got there
d) he struck the rock for water instead of speaking to it

Question #5

When Miriam spoke against Moses, she was struck with leprosy for:

a) 40 days
b) 7 days

c) the rest of her life
d) 1 year

Question #6

Who thought the king was going to honor him and instead ended up having to honor his worst enemy?

a) Haman
b) Mordecai

c) Absalom
d) Ahab

Question #7

Why did the Lord finally reject Saul from being king?

    a) Saul prophesied with the prophets
    b) Saul tried to kill David
    c) Saul rejected the word of the Lord
    d) Saul went to the witch of Endor

Question #8

When Elisha's servant lied to Naaman and took gifts from him, the servant was struck with:

    a) blindness   c) muteness
    b) deafness   d) Naaman's leprosy

Question #9

When Nebuchadnezzar claimed glory instead of giving the glory to God, he became mad and:

    a) tore his clothes
    b) lived like a wild animal
    c) lived in a cave
    d) both b and c

Question #10

When Herod allowed the people to say that his voice was the voice of a god, the angel of the Lord struck him:

    a) blind   c) mute
    b) deaf   d) dead

Humbling Experiences

ANSWERS

1. b) David (2 Samuel 12:7)

2. d) the law of his land said he couldn't (Daniel 6:7–15)

3. b) 2 (Mark 14:72)

4. d) he struck the rock for water instead of speaking to it (Numbers 20:7–12)

5. b) 7 days (Numbers 12:1–2, 14–15)

6. a) Haman (Esther 6:6–11)

7. c) Saul rejected the word of the Lord (1 Samuel 15:26)

8. d) Naaman's leprosy (2 Kings 5:20–27)

9. b) lived like a wild animal (Daniel 4:24–25, 30–33)

10. d) dead (Acts 12:20–23)

Did you outsmart the Sunday schoolers?

Can You Outsmart a Sunday Schooler?

When studying the Bible, it helps to understand the geography of the Middle East. Many places are very important to biblical history. The Bible says that unless the Lord keeps the city, the watchman walks in vain (Psalm 127:1). Some of the following cities were dedicated to the Lord, and some tried to exist without Him. Which of these cities do you recognize?

Question #1

The city of Babel and the city of Nineveh were both built by:

a) Adam
b) Seth
c) Cain
d) Nimrod

Question #2

Of the following four cities, which *two* were referred to as the city of David?

a) Zion
b) Bethlehem
c) Samaria
d) Shiloh

Question #3

Which of the following is *not* one of the foundation stones of the New Jerusalem?

a) sapphire
b) diamond
c) topaz
d) amethyst

Question #4

What prophet had a vision of a city whose name was "The Lord is there"?

- a) Ezekiel
- b) Jeremiah
- c) Isaiah
- d) Daniel

Question #5

The shortest sermon in the Bible consists of eight words: "Yet forty days, and _____ shall be overthrown." To what city was this sermon preached?

- a) Babylon
- b) Sodom
- c) Nineveh
- d) Gomorrah

Question #6

When Naomi returned from afar with Ruth, to which city did they go?

- a) Jerusalem
- b) Nazareth
- c) Jericho
- d) Bethlehem

Question #7

Which of the following was *not* a city that Lot lived in?

- a) Sodom
- b) Gomorrah
- c) Zoar
- d) Ur

Question #8

Samson carried off the gates of the city of:

    a) Gaza
    b) Joppa
    c) Ashkelon
    d) Jericho

Question #9

What city was Saul traveling to when he was struck by the light of Jesus?

    a) Jerusalem
    b) Damascus
    c) Corinth
    d) Joppa

Question #10

In what city did Jesus speak to the woman at the well?

    a) Jericho
    b) Joppa
    c) Samaria
    d) Caesarea

Cities

ANSWERS

1. d) Nimrod (Genesis 10:8–11)

2. a) Zion (2 Samuel 5:7) and b) Bethlehem (Luke 2:4)

3. b) diamond (Revelation 21:19–20)

4. a) Ezekiel (Ezekiel 48:35)

5. c) Nineveh (Jonah 3:4)

6. d) Bethlehem (Ruth 1:11–19)

7. b) Gomorrah (Genesis 13:12; 19:22–23; 11:31)

8. a) Gaza (Judges 16:1–3)

9. b) Damascus (Acts 9:3–4)

10. c) Samaria (John 4:5–7)

Did you outsmart the Sunday schoolers?

Can You
Outsmart
a
Sunday
Schooler?

The Bible itself is the Word of God, and it describes the Word of God in many different ways. Each description helps us understand a different aspect of God's Word and how it relates to us. With which of the following descriptions are you familiar?

Question #1

There is one psalm in the Bible in which each verse contains a reference to God's Word as His law. That psalm is:

- a) Psalm 1
- b) Psalm 19
- c) Psalm 23
- d) Psalm 119

Question #2

In the parable of the sower, the Word of God is likened to:

- a) the sower
- b) fertilizer
- c) the seed
- d) the receptive ground

Question #3

In the list of the armor of God in Ephesians 6, the Word of God is the:

- a) breastplate
- b) helmet
- c) shield
- d) sword

Question #4

Which Gospel begins by saying the Word was in the beginning with God and was God?

a) Matthew   c) Luke

b) Mark   d) John

Question #5

Hebrews 4:12 says the Word of God is:

a) quick

b) powerful

c) sharper than a two-edged sword

d) all of the above

Question #6

Jeremiah 23:29 says the Word of God is like a:

a) fire

b) hammer

c) rock

d) both a and b

Question #7

Hebrews 11:3 says something was framed by the Word of God. What was it?

a) the worlds

b) the heavens

c) mankind

d) all of the above

Question #8

Psalm 119:105 says the Word of God is a:
- a) river
- b) lamp
- c) rock
- d) path

Question #9

The Bible says that the Word became flesh and:
- a) came to die
- b) dwelt among us
- c) came to earth
- d) was rejected

Question #10

God said that when His Word goes out,
it will not return:
- a) void
- b) again
- c) ever
- d) to heaven

The Word of God

ANSWERS

1. d) Psalm 119
2. c) the seed (Luke 8:11)
3. d) sword (Ephesians 6:17)
4. d) John (John 1:1)
5. d) all of the above
6. d) both a and b
7. a) the worlds
8. b) lamp
9. b) dwelt among us (John 1:14)
10. a) void (Isaiah 55:11)

Did you outsmart the Sunday schoolers?

Can You
Outsmart
a
Sunday
Schooler?

"Do not forget to entertain strangers, for by so doing some have unwittingly entertained angels" (Hebrews 13:2 NKJV). Angels appeared to various people in the Bible. Sometimes the people knew they were angels, sometimes not. Are you aware of the following angels?

Question #1

What man's donkey saw an angel and spoke?

a) Barak
b) Balak
c) Balaam
d) Belshazzar

Question #2

Which of the following did *not* see a host of angels?

a) Jacob
b) Peter
c) shepherds at Bethlehem
d) John

Question #3

What famous judge's parents saw an angel ascend to heaven in a flame?

a) Gideon
b) Deborah
c) Samson
d) Samuel

Question #4

The cherubim sent to keep people out of the Garden of Eden were placed on which side of the garden?

a) north   c) east
b) south   d) west

Question #5

To which of the following people did the angel Gabriel *not* appear?

a) Mary
b) Daniel
c) Zacharias
d) Paul

Question #6

In Revelation 10:6 an angel declared that:

a) the kingdom had come
b) Jesus is King of Kings
c) there should be time no longer
d) all of the above

Question #7

When Isaiah saw the seraphim, each one had how many wings?

a) 2
b) 4
c) 6
d) 8

Question #8

The angels carved on the top of the ark of the covenant were:

   a) cherubim
   b) seraphim
   c) both cherubim and seraphim
   d) neither cherubim nor seraphim

Question #9

How many angels went to save Lot from the destruction of his city?

   a) 2
   b) 4
   c) 8
   d) 10

Question #10

Hebrews 2:7 says that God made man:

   a) rulers over angels
   b) higher than the angels
   c) lower than the angels
   d) equal with the angels

Angels

ANSWERS

1. c) Balaam (Numbers 22:22–23)

2. b) Peter (Genesis 28:10–12;
   Luke 2:8–14; Revelation 7:11)

3. c) Samson (Judges 13:20, 24)

4. c) east (Genesis 3:24)

5. d) Paul (Luke 1:26–27; Daniel 8:15–16;
   Luke 1:18–19)

6. c) there should be time no longer

7. c) 6 (Isaiah 6:2)

8. a) cherubim (Exodus 37:1, 7)

9. a) 2 (Genesis 19:1)

10. c) lower than the angels

Did you outsmart
the Sunday schoolers?

Can You
Outsmart
a
Sunday
Schooler?

There's inevitably some stuff left over from all the other categories, so here we have a special miscellaneous quiz to catch the overflow. How many of these odd little facts do you know?

Question #1

What did God create first?
- a) light
- b) water
- c) time
- d) the heavens and the earth

Question #2

What does *sabbath* mean?
- a) "rest"
- b) "sleep"
- c) "feast"
- d) "holy"

Question #3

The word *manna* actually means:
- a) "bread from heaven"
- b) "round"
- c) "white"
- d) "What is it?"

Question #4

Who was born grasping his brother's heel?
- a) Abel
- b) Shem
- c) Jacob
- d) Esau

Question #5

The first song in the Bible and the last song in the Bible were written by the same person. Who?
- a) Jesus
- b) an angel
- c) Abraham
- d) Moses

Question #6

Which of the following groups was anointed?
- a) cleansed lepers
- b) prophets
- c) priests
- d) all of the above

Question #7

Who of the following was *not* a shepherd?
- a) David
- b) Abel
- c) Amos
- d) Isaiah

Question #8

Who was so short that he climbed up into a sycamore tree to see Jesus?

    a)   Zephaniah
    b)   Zechariah
    c)   Zadok
    d)   Zacchaeus

Question #9

What sign did God give Noah as a promise that He would never again flood the earth?

    a)   a cross
    b)   a rainbow
    c)   an altar
    d)   a tablet

Question #10

When Jesus was baptized, the Holy Spirit descended upon Him like a:

    a)   dove
    b)   ray of light
    c)   feather
    d)   bolt of lightning

Miscellaneous

ANSWERS

1. d) the heavens and the earth
   (Genesis 1:1)

2. a) "rest"

3. d) "What is it?" (Exodus 16:15 NKJV)

4. c) Jacob (Genesis 25:26)

5. d) Moses (Exodus 15:1;
   Revelation 15:3)

6. d) all of the above (Leviticus 14:15–18;
   1 Kings 19:16; Exodus 28:41)

7. d) Isaiah (1 Samuel 16:11–13;
   Genesis 4:2; Amos 1:1)

8. d) Zaccheus (Luke 19:2–4)

9. b) a rainbow (Genesis 9:13)

10. a) dove (Matthew 3:16)

Did you outsmart
the Sunday schoolers?

Can You
Outsmart
a
Sunday
Schooler?

Only two books of the Bible are named for women. Like all of the Bible's stories, these two stories are important. What do you know about these two extraordinary women?

Question #1

Ruth was from:
- a) Edom
- b) Moab
- c) Ammon
- d) Tyre

Question #2

Ruth's mother-in-law was:
- a) Naomi
- b) Orpah
- c) Rahab
- d) both a and c

Question #3

Boaz was Naomi's:
- a) son
- b) kinsman
- c) brother-in-law
- d) cousin

Question #4

When Boaz first saw Ruth, she was:
- a) cooking
- b) washing clothes
- c) planting a garden
- d) gleaning

Question #5

In order to show that he would allow Boaz to marry Ruth, the other man:
- a) shook hands
- b) winked
- c) took off his shoe
- d) turned in a circle three times

Question #6

The name of the queen before Esther was:
- a) Vashti
- b) Jezebel
- c) Sheba
- d) Candace

Question #7

If someone went to King Ahasuerus unannounced, he or she would be killed unless the king:
- a) smiled
- b) said to leave him or her alone
- c) held out his scepter
- d) motioned with his hand

Question #8

Haman was:
- a) a king
- b) a prince
- c) the king's second in command
- d) a chamberlain

Question #9

In order to expose Haman's plot, Esther:
- a) threw herself at the king's feet
- b) invited the king and Haman to a banquet
- c) got Mordecai an audience with the king
- d) a and b

Question #10

A feast was instituted to celebrate the defeat of Haman's plot. It was called the feast of:
- a) Tabernacles
- b) Esther
- c) Purim
- d) Mordecai

Ruth and Esther

ANSWERS

1. b) Moab (Ruth 1:4)

2. d) both a and c (Ruth 1:2–4; Matthew 1:5)

3. b) kinsman (Ruth 2:1)

4. d) gleaning (Ruth 2:2–4)

5. c) took off his shoe (Ruth 4:8)

6. a) Vashti (Esther 1:9)

7. c) held out his scepter (Esther 4:11)

8. c) the king's second in command (Esther 3:1)

9. b) invited the king and Haman to a banquet (Esther 5:7–8)

10. c) Purim (Esther 9:26)

Did you outsmart the Sunday schoolers?

Can You
Outsmart
a
Sunday
Schooler?

Mountains are plentiful in the geography of the Bible. Many important events took place on or near a mountain. Which of these mountains and events are you familiar with?

Question #1

God gave Moses the Ten Commandments on Mount:

  a) Sinai   c) Moriah

  b) Pisgah   d) Zion

Question #2

Elijah called down fire from heaven to defeat the prophets of Baal on what mountain?

  a) Horeb

  b) Carmel

  c) Hor

  d) Moriah

Question #3

When God showed Moses all of the Promised Land, He took Moses up on Mount:

  a) Sinai

  b) Horeb

  c) Pisgah

  d) Moriah

Question #4

When God tested Abraham, He told Abraham to take Isaac up on Mount:

a) Zion
b) Moriah
c) Horeb
d) Sinai

Question #5

The Garden of Gethsemane was on:

a) the Mount of Olives
b) Mount Hermon
c) Mount Calvary
d) Mount Zion

Question #6

Which of the following mountains was called the "mountain of God" or the "mount [or "mountain"] of the Lord"?

a) Zion
b) Sinai
c) Horeb
d) all of the above

Question #7

Mount Calvary is also called Golgotha, which means:

a) "death"
b) "burning"
c) "shame"
d) "skull"

Question #8

Jesus was transfigured on:
   a) Mount Calvary
   b) a high mountain
   c) the Mount of Olives
   d) Mount Zion

Question #9

Upon what mountain was Moses when he saw the burning bush?
   a) Sinai
   b) Horeb
   c) Tabor
   d) Midian

Question #10

Which of the following tribes of Israel had a mountain named for it?
   a) Reuben
   b) Gad
   c) Ephraim
   d) Dan

Mountains

ANSWERS

1. a) Sinai (Exodus 19:18–20:17)

2. b) Carmel (1 Kings 18:19, 30–38)

3. c) Pisgah (Deuteronomy 34:1–4)

4. b) Moriah (Genesis 22:1–2)

5. a) the Mount of Olives
(Matthew 26:36; Luke 22:39)

6. d) all of the above (Isaiah 2:3;
Numbers 10:12, 33; Exodus 3:1)

7. d) "skull" (Matthew 27:33)

8. b) a high mountain (Matthew 17:1)

9. b) Horeb (Exodus 3:1–4)

10. c) Ephraim (1 Samuel 1:1)

Did you outsmart
the Sunday schoolers?

Can You
Outsmart
a
Sunday
Schooler?

Romans 10:13 says, "Whosoever shall call upon the name of the Lord shall be saved." The Lord tells us many of His different names because each of His names speaks to a different aspect of His character. Knowing His names helps us to know God better. How well do you know these names of the Lord?

Question #1

To whom was God speaking when He said, "Say unto the children of Israel, I AM hath sent me unto you"?

a) Aaron   c) Joshua

b) Moses   d) Elijah

Question #2

Who called the Lord "Thou God seest me"?

a) Sarai

b) Abram

c) Hagar

d) Ishmael

Question #3

To whom was God speaking when He said, "I am the Almighty God"?

a) Moses

b) Aaron

c) Abram

d) Pharaoh

Question #4

When Moses told the children of Israel to remember the days of old, he referred to the Lord as:

    a)   the Most High
    b)   the Ancient of Days
    c)   the Lord of Lords
    d)   the Lord above all

Question #5

Which of the Ten Commandments tells us not to take our Lord's name in vain?

    a)   1   c)   3
    b)   2   d)   4

Question #6

Which of the following names is not in the list found in Isaiah 9:6?

    a)   Bright and Morning Star
    b)   Prince of Peace
    c)   Mighty God
    d)   Counsellor

Question #7

"KING OF KINGS, AND LORD OF LORDS" was written on Jesus':

    a)   vesture and thigh
    b)   shield
    c)   sword
    d)   breastplate

Question #8

Which of the following names means
"God with us"?

   a) Jesus
   b) Elohim
   c) Emmanuel
   d) Elyon

Question #9

Philippians 2:9 says that God gave Jesus:

   a) the name Jesus
   b) the name above every name
   c) a secret name
   d) b and c

Question #10

Who said, "I know that my Redeemer lives"?

   a) David
   b) Job
   c) Moses
   d) Isaiah

Names of the Lord

ANSWERS

1. b) Moses (Exodus 3:14)

2. c) Hagar (Genesis 16:8, 13)

3. c) Abram (Genesis 17:1)

4. a) the Most High
   (Deuteronomy 31:30; 32:8)

5. c) 3 (Exodus 20:7)

6. a) Bright and Morning Star

7. a) vesture and thigh
   (Revelation 19:16)

8. c) Emmanuel (Matthew 1:23)

9. b) the name above every name

10. b) Job (Job 19:1, 25 NKJV)

Did you outsmart
the Sunday schoolers?

Can You
Outsmart
a
Sunday
Schooler?

Jesus' Crucifixion and Resurrection

Galatians 2:20 says, "I am crucified with Christ: nevertheless I live; yet not I, but Christ liveth in me." Christ's crucifixion and resurrection are the most important events ever to happen in this world. What do you know about these crucial events?

Question #1

The week before His crucifixion, Jesus entered Jerusalem and was greeted with:

a) hosannas
b) strewn garments
c) branches of trees
d) all of the above

Question #2

Jesus was betrayed with a:

a) handshake
b) pointing finger
c) slap in the face
d) kiss

Question #3

Jesus was tried before:

a) Caiaphas
b) Pilate
c) Herod
d) all of the above

Question #4

Who helped Jesus to carry His cross?
- a) Peter
- b) a Roman soldier
- c) Simon of Cyrene
- d) a slave

Question #5

The sign Pilate put on Jesus' cross said "The King of the Jews" in how many languages?

- a) 1
- b) 2
- c) 3
- d) 4

Question #6

Who gave his tomb for Jesus to be buried in?
- a) Nicodemus
- b) Joseph of Arimathea
- c) Peter
- d) Lazarus

Question #7

How many Marys were standing at the foot of the cross?

- a) 1
- b) 2
- c) 3
- d) 4

Question #8

Who came first to the tomb on the first day of the week?

    a) Peter
    b) John
    c) Mary, Jesus' mother
    d) Mary Magdalene

Question #9

Who rolled the stone away?

    a) an angel
    b) the women
    c) Jesus' disciples
    d) Roman soldiers

Question #10

What was left in the tomb?

    a) nothing
    b) the linen clothes
    c) some spices
    d) an angel

Jesus' Crucifixion and Resurrection

ANSWERS

1. d) all of the above (Matthew 21:8–9)

2. d) kiss (Matthew 26:49)

3. d) all of the above (Matthew 26:57; 27:11–13; Luke 23:7)

4. c) Simon of Cyrene (Matthew 27:32)

5. c) 3 (Luke 23:38; John 19:19)

6. b) Joseph of Arimathea (Matthew 27:57–60)

7. c) 3 (John 19:25)

8. d) Mary Magdalene (John 20:1)

9. a) an angel (Matthew 28:2)

10. b) the linen clothes (John 20:6)

Did you outsmart the Sunday schoolers?

Can You
Outsmart
a
Sunday
Schooler?

God instituted the priesthood. He chose the tribe of Levi because they were the only ones who stood with Moses to punish those worshipping the golden calf. The only book of the Bible named for a tribe of Israel is Leviticus, which describes the duties of the priests. Today we Christians are God's royal priesthood. What do you know about the biblical priests?

Question #1

When Samuel was dedicated to service in the house of the Lord, the priest he served was:

a) Zadok
b) Eli

c) Eleazar
d) Melchizedek

Question #2

When Aaron died, what was the name of his son who became high priest?

a) Eleazar
b) Phinehas

c) Joshua
d) Caleb

Question #3

Melchizedek was a priest of:

a) Jerusalem
b) Baal
c) the most high God
d) Israel

Question #4

Which apostle wrote a book of the Bible that describes all believers as a royal priesthood?

a) Paul
b) Peter
c) James
d) John

Question #5

When the Israelites returned to Jerusalem from the Babylonian captivity, the high priest was:

a) Ezra
b) Nehemiah
c) Joshua
d) Zerubbabel

Question #6

David put the two priests Abiathar and Zadok in charge of:

a) the temple service
b) bringing the ark of the covenant to Jerusalem
c) the temple singers
d) all the other priests

Question #7

Hebrews says that Jesus is our High Priest forever according to the order of:

a) Moses
b) Aaron
c) Levi
d) Melchizedek

Question #8

In Jesus' day a curious situation occurred in which two men were referred to as being the high priest. The two men were:

- a) Annas and Caiaphas
- b) Caiaphas and Zecharias
- c) Annas and Zecharias
- d) Caiaphas and Gamaliel

Question #9

Which of the following was *not* a part of what the priests were to wear?

- a) ephod
- b) turban
- c) breastplate
- d) gloves

Question #10

How often could the high priest enter the Holy of Holies, where the ark of the covenant was?

- a) once a year
- b) on holy feast days
- c) on the sabbath
- d) twice a year

Priests

ANSWERS

1. b) Eli (1 Samuel 1:20–25)

2. a) Eleazar (Deuteronony 10:6)

3. c) the most high God (Genesis 14:18)

4. b) Peter (1 Peter 2:9)

5. c) Joshua (Haggai 1:1–2)

6. b) bringing the ark of the covenant to Jeruselem (2 Samuel 15:29)

7. d) Melchizedek (Hebrews 6:20)

8. a) Annas and Caiaphas (Luke 3:2)

9. d) gloves (Exodus 28:4–39)

10. a) once a year (Hebrews 9:6–7)

Did you outsmart the Sunday schoolers?

Can You
Outsmart
a
Sunday
Schooler?

Plagues

When God was ready to deliver His people from slavery in Egypt, He sent Moses to Pharaoh. But Pharaoh refused to let God's people go. Some scholars say that each of the plagues was directed against a specific Egyptian god or goddess so that God could show His supremacy over all phony gods. What do you know about the plagues? Can you name all ten plagues?

Question #1

Which of the following plagues did the Egyptian magicians *not* duplicate?

    a) water to blood
    b) rods turned into snakes
    c) frogs
    d) lice

Question #2

How many plagues did God send against the Egyptians?

    a) 10
    b) 12
    c) 13
    d) 9

Question #3

In order to have the angel of death leave their firstborn alive, the Israelites anointed their doorposts and lintels with:

a) hyssop

b) myrrh

c) blood

d) frankincense

Question #4

Which of the following plagues is *not* paralleled in the plagues of the tribulation in the book of Revelation?

a) locusts

b) darkness

c) hail and fire

d) boils

Question #5

Out of the following list, which plague occurred first?

a) boils

b) flies

c) frogs

d) locusts

Question #6

God told Aaron to stretch out his rod so that the dust of the land would become:

a) locusts

b) flies

c) a cloud of darkness

d) lice

Question #7

The Bible repeatedly says that Pharaoh:
- a) loved his power
- b) closed his mind
- c) hardened his heart
- d) closed his ears

Question #8

The last plague—death of the firstborn—resulted in what major celebration for the Israelites?
- a) the Day of Atonement
- b) the Feast of Tabernacles
- c) Passover
- d) the Feast of Trumpets

Question #9

God visited the plagues upon Egypt:
- a) because He was angry at the Egyptians
- b) because He was angry with Pharaoh
- c) so that the Egyptians would know that He is Lord
- d) because He could

Question #10

How many days did the plague of darkness last?
- a) 1
- b) 2
- c) 3
- d) 4

Plagues

ANSWERS

1. d) lice (Exodus 8:16–19)

2. a) 10 (Exodus 7:20; 8:6, 17, 24;
       9:6, 10, 23; 10:13, 22; 12:29)

3. c) blood (Exodus 12:7, 13)

4. d) boils (Revelation 8:7; 9:2–3)

5. c) frogs (Exodus 8:2)

6. d) lice (Exodus 8:16)

7. c) hardened his heart (Exodus 8:15, 32;
       9:34; 10:1; 11:10)

8. c) Passover (Exodus 12:13–14)

9. c) so that the Egyptians would know
       that He is Lord (Exodus 7:5)

10. c) 3 (Exodus 10:22)

Did you outsmart
the Sunday schoolers?

Can You Outsmart a Sunday Schooler?

According to Hebrews 8:5, God told Moses to make the tabernacle according to the pattern shown to him on the mount. As Christians, we can learn much by comparing the utensils of the tabernacle to their symbolic references—light, bread, mercy; everything points to Jesus. The temple was patterned after the tabernacle but as a permanent dwelling. How much do you know about the tabernacle and the temple?

Question #1

Which of the following was *not* one of the colors of the tabernacle curtains?

a) blue
b) red
c) purple
d) white

Question #2

Which of the following was *not* placed in the Holy of Holies?

a) table of showbread
b) altar of incense
c) a bronze basin for washing
d) golden lampstand

Question #3

Who carried the tabernacle and its furnishings?

a) the Levites
b) the Gadites
c) the Reubenites
d) the Ephraimites

Question #4

When the Israelites camped, the tabernacle was set up:

a) to the north of the camp
b) to the south of the camp
c) to the east of the camp
d) in the middle of the camp

Question #5

The glory of the Lord filled the tabernacle as:

a) a pillar of cloud
b) a pillar of fire
c) lightning
d) both a and b

Question #6

Who built the first temple?

a) Moses
b) Solomon
c) Samuel
d) Hezekiah

Question #7

When David wanted to build a temple, why did God tell him he couldn't?

a) because he didn't have the right building materials
b) because he sinned with Bathsheba
c) because he had shed much blood
d) because he was too old

Question #8

According to 1 Chronicles 22:1–5, which of the following was *not* a material gathered to build the temple?

- a) iron
- b) brass (or bronze)
- c) stone
- d) gold

Question #9

Jesus cleansed the temple of:

- a) money changers
- b) animals
- c) Pharisees
- d) priests

Question #10

When Jesus died, the veil in the temple was torn in two from:

- a) bottom to top
- b) top to bottom
- c) right to left
- d) left to right

Tabernacle and Temple

ANSWERS

1. d) white (Exodus 26:1)

2. c) a bronze basin for washing
   (Exodus 30:18)

3. a) Levites (Numbers 1:50)

4. d) in the middle of the camp
   (Numbers 2:17)

5. d) both a and b (Exodus 40:38)

6. b) Solomon (2 Chronicles 2:1)

7. c) because he had shed much blood
   (1 Chronicles 22:8)

8. d) gold

9. a) money changers (Matthew 21:12)

10. b) top to bottom (Mark 15:38)

Did you outsmart
the Sunday schoolers?

Can You
Outsmart
a
Sunday
Schooler?

In addition to quoting familiar verses, a lot of people can quote familiar Bible stories or scripture passages. Do you know where the following are found?

Question #1

Which two books of the New Testament record what we know as "the Lord's Prayer"?

a) Matthew and Luke
b) Matthew and Mark
c) Matthew and John
d) Matthew and Acts

Question #2

What verse in the Bible is commonly referred to as "the Golden Rule"?

a) John 3:16
b) Matthew 7:12
c) Luke 2:52
d) Mark 16:18

Question #3

Where is the description of the virtuous woman?

a) Psalm 19
b) Ecclesiastes 3
c) Proverbs 31
d) Song of Solomon 1

Question #4

What book of the Bible is characterized by the phrase "vanity of vanities; all is vanity"?

 a) Job   c) Micah
 b) Ecclesiastes d) Hosea

Question #5

What book of the Bible contains the story of David and Goliath?

 a) 1 Samuel
 b) 2 Samuel
 c) 1 Kings
 d) 2 Kings

Question #6

What book of the Bible contains the story of Noah and the flood?

 a) Genesis
 b) Exodus
 c) Leviticus
 d) Numbers

Question #7

The story of the prodigal son is in which Gospel?

 a) Matthew
 b) Mark
 c) Luke
 d) John

Question #8

Where can you find the saying "They shall beat their swords into plowshares"?

a) Job 40:1
b) Jeremiah 1:5
c) Amos 3:3
d) Isaiah 2:4

Question #9

Where can we find the foolish man building his house upon the sand?

a) Matthew 7:26
b) Mark 7:26
c) Luke 7:26
d) John 7:26

Question #10

Where is the story of Moses in the bulrushes?

a) Exodus 1
b) Exodus 2
c) Exodus 3
d) Exodus 4

Where Is This Found?

ANSWERS

1. a) Matthew and Luke
   (Matthew 6:9–13; Luke 11:2–4)

2. b) Matthew 7:12

3. c) Proverbs 31

4. b) Ecclesiastes 1:2; 12:8

5. a) 1 Samuel 17

6. a) Genesis 6–9

7. c) Luke 15:11–32

8. d) Isaiah 2:4

9. a) Matthew 7:26

10. b) Exodus 2:2–8

Did you outsmart the Sunday schoolers?

Can You
Outsmart
a
Sunday
Schooler?

Everything Jesus said was well worth listening to. He spoke to many thousands of people, but He also spoke to individuals. Jesus was compassionate, kind, loving, and informative. To whom was Jesus speaking when He made the following statements?

Question #1

"Suffer the little children to come unto me, and forbid them not."

a) their parents
b) His disciples
c) the Pharisees
d) the crowd

Question #2

"Whosoever liveth and believeth in me shall never die. Believest thou this?"

a) Mary Magdalene
b) the woman at the well
c) Martha
d) His mother

Question #3

"Woman, why weepest thou?"

a) His mother
b) Mary, the sister of Lazarus
c) Martha
d) Mary Magdalene

Question #4

"Woman, what have I to do with thee?"

 a) the woman at the well
 b) the woman with an issue of blood
 c) Pilate's wife
 d) His mother

Question #5

"Why are you persecuting Me?"

 a) the high priest
 b) the Pharisees
 c) Satan
 d) Saul

Question #6

"What is that to thee? follow thou me."

 a) Peter
 b) Andrew
 c) James
 d) John

Question #7

"Why do you call Me good?"

 a) Matthew
 b) Nathaniel
 c) the rich young ruler
 d) Nicodemus

Question #8

"God is a Spirit: and they that worship him must worship him in spirit and in truth."

    a)   the Pharisees
    b)   His disciples
    c)   the woman at the well
    d)   Pilate

Question #9

"Wist ye not that I must be about my Father's business?"

    a)   His disciples
    b)   His parents
    c)   Mary and Martha
    d)   Philip

Question #10

"That thou doest, do quickly."

    a)   Peter
    b)   John
    c)   Judas
    d)   Caiaphas

Jesus Speaking

ANSWERS

1. b) His disciples (Mark 10:13–14)
2. c) Martha (John 11:24, 26)
3. d) Mary Magdalene (John 20:1, 15)
4. d) His mother (John 2:3–4)
5. d) Saul (Acts 9:4 NKJV)
6. a) Peter (John 21:21–22)
7. c) the rich young ruler (Matthew 19:17 NKJV; Luke 18:18–19 NKJV)
8. c) the woman at the well (John 4:7, 24)
9. b) His parents (Luke 2:41, 49)
10. c) Judas (John 13:26–27)

Did you outsmart the Sunday schoolers?

Can You
Outsmart
a
Sunday
Schooler?

Hebrews 11:6 says that without faith it is impossible to please God. All of the following people could say with the apostle Paul, "I have fought a good fight, I have finished my course, I have kept the faith" (2 Timothy 4:7). What do you know about these faithful of God?

Question #1

Of whom does the Bible say, "In all this _____ sinned not, nor charged God foolishly"?

    a) Nehemiah   c) John
    b) Job   d) Moses

Question #2

Shadrach, Meshach, and Abednego were thrown into the fiery furnace because they refused to:

    a) pray to the king
    b) bow down to the king's statue
    c) stop praying to their God
    d) all of the above

Question #3

About whom is the Bible speaking when it says that among men whose thoughts were only evil continually, this person found grace in the eyes of the Lord?

    a) Noah   c) David
    b) Abraham   d) Moses

Question #4

About whom was God speaking when He said, "He has a different spirit in him and has followed Me fully"?

- a) Job
- b) Caleb
- c) David
- d) Moses

Question #5

Which of the following is *not* listed by name in Hebrews 11, God's hall of fame for His faithful?

- a) Abel
- b) Joseph
- c) Rahab
- d) Elijah

Question #6

About which of Noah's ancestors does the Bible say he "walked with God" and "God took him"?

- a) Seth
- b) Methuselah
- c) Enoch
- d) Lamech

Question #7

When Abraham proved his faithfulness to God by preparing to sacrifice Isaac, what did God provide as a sacrifice instead?

- a) a lamb
- b) a bullock
- c) a ram
- d) a goat

Question #8

About whom did Jesus say, "I have not found so great faith, no, not in Israel"?
- a) John the Baptist
- b) the centurion with the sick servant
- c) Jarius
- d) the man with the demon-possessed son

Question #9

How many years did Noah spend preparing the ark as God told him?
- a) 10
- b) 50
- c) 75
- d) 100

Question #10

What prophet who devoutly feared God hid one hundred prophets from Jezebel?
- a) Elijah
- b) Elisha
- c) Obadiah
- d) Isaiah

God's Faithful

ANSWERS

1. b) Job (Job 1:22)

2. b) bow down to the king's statue
       (Daniel 3:12)

3. a) Noah (Genesis 6:5, 8)

4. b) Caleb (Numbers 14:24 NKJV)

5. d) Elijah

6. c) Enoch (Genesis 5:24)

7. c) a ram (Genesis 22:13)

8. b) the centurion with the sick servant
       (Matthew 8:5, 10–14)

9. d) 100 (Genesis 5:32; 7:11)

10. c) Obadiah (1 Kings 18:3–4)

Did you outsmart
the Sunday schoolers?

Can You
Outsmart
a
Sunday
Schooler?

The book of Acts is sometimes called the Acts of the Apostles because that's what it describes. How many of the following acts are you familiar with?

Question #1

On the day of Pentecost, who preached the sermon?

    a)   John

    b)   Peter

    c)   Andrew

    d)   James

Question #2

On the day of Pentecost, the Holy Spirit appeared as:

    a)   a dove

    b)   tongues of fire

    c)   a lightning bolt

    d)   a mighty wind

Question #3

When Peter told Ananias and Sapphira that they had lied to the Holy Spirit, their punishment was:

    a)   banishment

    b)   flogging

    c)   confession to the whole church

    d)   death

Question #4

The first person martyred for being a Christian was:

    a) Philip
    b) Peter
    c) Stephen
    d) Paul

Question #5

Simon, who tried to buy the gift of the Holy Spirit, was a:

    a) king
    b) councilman
    c) sorcerer
    d) priest

Question #6

The apostle who spoke to the Ethiopian eunuch was:

    a) Peter
    b) Philip
    c) Paul
    d) Andrew

Question #7

Peter was sent to preach to Cornelius, who was a:

    a) Gentile   c) centurion
    b) devout man   d) all of the above

Question #8

When Peter was freed from prison by an angel and went to where the Christians had gathered, he was:

    a) welcomed
    b) left knocking at the door
    c) turned away
    d) ignored

Question #9

The apostle chosen to replace Judas was:

    a) Paul
    b) Silas
    c) Barnabas
    d) Matthias

Question #10

Lydia, who was one of the women converted at Philippi, was a seller of:

    a) purple
    b) pottery
    c) rich clothing
    d) housewares

The Acts of the Apostles

ANSWERS

1. b) Peter (Acts 2:1, 14)

2. b) tongues of fire (Acts 2:1, 3)

3. d) death (Acts 5:1–10)

4. c) Stephen (Acts 7:59)

5. c) sorcerer (Acts 8:9, 18)

6. b) Philip (Acts 8:26–35)

7. d) all of the above (Acts 10:1–2)

8. b) left knocking at the door (Acts 12:6–16)

9. d) Matthias (Acts 1:20–26)

10. a) purple (Acts 16:14)

Did you outsmart the Sunday schoolers?

Can You
Outsmart
a
Sunday
Schooler?

Jesus said that He spoke in parables to fulfill the prophecy of Isaiah that said the people would hear and not understand (Isaiah 6:9). The parables teach many good lessons, but we have to be willing to be taught. What do you know about these parables?

Question #1

The parable of the good Samaritan was told to answer what question?

    a)   "Who is my neighbor?"
    b)   "What shall I do to inherit eternal life?"
    c)   "Can a rich man be saved?"
    d)   "By what authority do you do these things?"

Question #2

The phrase "Well done, thou good and faithful servant" occurs in the parable of the:

    a)   sower
    b)   talents
    c)   minas
    d)   vineyard

Question #3

The parable of the unforgiving servant begins with Jesus saying that we should forgive:
   a)   a hundred times
   b)   seventy times seven
   c)   always
   d)   seven times

Question #4

In the parable of the lost sheep, how many sheep did the shepherd leave to search for the lost one?
   a)   9
   b)   99
   c)   199
   d)   299

Question #5

In the parable of the sower, upon how many different types of places did the seed fall?
   a)   3
   b)   4
   c)   5
   d)   7

Question #6

Which parable has the phrase "eat, drink, and be merry"?
   a)   Lazarus and the rich man
   b)   the rich fool
   c)   the rich young ruler
   d)   the wise steward

Question #7

In the parable of the wise and foolish virgins, how many took no oil with them?

    a) 3   c) 7
    b) 5   d) 9

Question #8

In the parable of the wedding feast, the man is thrown out because:

    a) he's not wearing a wedding garment
    b) he sat in the place of honor uninvited
    c) he wasn't invited to the wedding
    d) he was rude to the bridegroom

Question #9

In the parable of the wheat and tares, the owner of the field ultimately tells his servants to:

    a) root out the tares
    b) leave the tares alone
    c) bind the tares and burn them
    d) sow more tares

Question #10

In one parable Jesus said that no one would light a candle and:

    a) hide it under a bushel
    b) put it in a secret place
    c) let someone blow it out
    d) both a and b

Parables

ANSWERS

1. a) "Who is my neighbor?" (Luke 10:29)

2. b) talents (Matthew 25:21)

3. b) seventy times seven
(Matthew 18:22)

4. b) 99 (Matthew 18:12)

5. b) 4 (Mark 4:3–8)

6. b) the rich fool (Luke 12:19)

7. b) 5 (Matthew 25:2)

8. a) he's not wearing a wedding
garment (Matthew 22:11–12)

9. c) bind the tares and burn them
(Matthew 13:30)

10. d) both a and b (Luke 11:33)

Did you outsmart
the Sunday schoolers?

Can You Outsmart a Sunday Schooler?

As part of His ministry, Jesus performed miracles. One reason was to prove He was who He said He was—the Son of God. But another reason was to show His love and compassion for His people. What do you know about these miracles?

Question #1

After Jesus fed the 5,000, He fed another group of 4,000 with:

    a) 5 loaves and 2 fish
    b) 6 loaves and 3 fish
    c) 7 loaves and a few fish
    d) 8 loaves and no fish

Question #2

When the 4,000 were finished eating, how many baskets full were left over?

    a) 3   c) 7
    b) 5   d) 12

Question #3

When Jesus walked on water, which disciple asked to get out of the boat and walk to Jesus on the water?

    a) Peter   c) John
    b) James   d) Thomas

Question #4

How long was Lazarus dead before Jesus raised him up again?

a) a few hours

b) 1 day

c) 4 days

d) 7 days

Question #5

Jesus turned the water to wine at:

a) Passover

b) the Last Supper

c) a wedding

d) both a and c

Question #6

When Jesus healed the ten lepers, how many returned to thank Him?

a) 10

b) 5

c) 9

d) 1

Question #7

When the friends of the paralyzed man couldn't get their friend to Jesus because of the crowd, they:

a) lowered him down through the roof

b) stood on the edge of the crowd and shouted

c) gave up and went away

d) pushed their way through the crowd

Question #8

When Jesus healed the man who was blind from birth, what did He put on the man's eyes?

    a)   clay
    b)   His hand
    c)   a scarf
    d)   nothing

Question #9

The crippled man Jesus healed at the pool of Bethesda was at the pool because:

    a)   the waters were healing
    b)   an angel sometimes appeared
    c)   it was where he lived
    d)   a and b

Question #10

Jesus once caused a tree to wither to prove a point. What kind of tree was it?

    a)   olive
    b)   fig
    c)   sycamore
    d)   palm

Miracles of Jesus

ANSWERS

1. c) 7 loaves and a few fish
   (Matthew 15:34–38)

2. c) 7 (Matthew 15:37–38)

3. a) Peter (Matthew 14:24–29)

4. c) 4 days (John 11:14, 39)

5. c) a wedding (John 2:1–10)

6. d) 1 (Luke 17:12–16)

7. a) lowered him down through the
   roof (Mark 2:4)

8. a) clay (John 9:1, 6)

9. d) both a and b (John 5:2–9)

10. b) fig (Mark 11:14, 20)

Did you outsmart
the Sunday schoolers?

Can You

Outsmart

a

Sunday

Schooler?

Revelation

The book of Revelation starts by saying it is a revelation of Jesus Christ given to His servant John. Revelation is full of symbols and strange things that God uses to show Himself to us. How much do you know about this book of the Bible?

Question #1

Revelation begins with messages to how many churches?

a) 3
b) 5

c) 7
d) 9

Question #2

The churches are likened to:

a) stars
b) lampstands
c) bread
d) salt

Question #3

Out of the following things, which did John see first?

a) seals
b) trumpets
c) bowls of God's wrath
d) censers

Question #4

John saw four horses. The last one was pale and the name of him who rode it was:

    a) Hades
    b) Apollyon
    c) Death
    d) Famine

Question #5

The 144,000 were:

    a) those with the mark of the beast
    b) God's servants
    c) angels
    d) martyrs

Question #6

How many witnesses did God send?

    a) 1
    b) 2
    c) 3
    d) 4

Question #7

What happened to God's witnesses?

    a) they were killed and resurrected
    b) nothing
    c) nobody would listen to them
    d) they ascended into heaven

Question #8

How many beasts stood around God's throne?

    a) 2
    b) 4
    c) 6
    d) 24

Question #9

How many elders were before the throne?

    a) 12
    b) 24
    c) 36
    d) 48

Question #10

What did John see descend from the new heaven?

    a) a new earth
    b) a new sea
    c) the new Jerusalem
    d) the new army of God

Revelation

ANSWERS

1. c) 7 (Revelation 1:4)

2. b) lampstands (Revelation 1:20)

3. a) seals (Revelation 6:1)

4. c) Death (Revelation 6:8)

5. b) God's servants (Revelation 7:3–4)

6. b) 2 (Revelation 11:3)

7. a) they were killed and resurrected
   (Revelation 11:3, 7, 11)

8. b) 4 (Revelation 4:6)

9. b) 24 (Revelation 4:10)

10. c) the new Jerusalem
    (Revelation 21:1–2)

Did you outsmart
the Sunday schoolers?

Can You
Outsmart
a
Sunday
Schooler?

The Bible is full of significant numbers. Some numbers we see repeated over and over, like the numbers 40 and 7. There is even a book called Numbers. What do you know about the following numbers? (You won't need a calculator, we promise!)

Question #1

How many prophesying daughters did Philip have?

    a) 1   c) 3

    b) 2   d) 4

Question #2

How many were added to the church on the day of Pentecost?

    a) 1,000

    b) 2,000

    c) 3,000

    d) 5,000

Question #3

How many foxtails did Samson tie together and put firebrands between to burn up his enemies' fields?

    a) 100

    b) 200

    c) 300

    d) 500

Question #4

How many years were the children of Israel in Egypt?
    a) 120
    b) 360
    c) 430
    d) 520

Question #5

What was the final count of men in Gideon's army?
    a) 300
    b) 3,000
    c) 3,300
    d) 10,000

Question #6

After Noah finished the ark, how many days and nights did it rain?

    a) 7   c) 40
    b) 10   d) 100

Question #7

How old was Methuselah when he died?
    a) 939
    b) 949
    c) 959
    d) 969

Question #8

How many cities were the Levites given as their inheritance in the Promised Land?

   a)   12
   b)   24
   c)   36
   d)   48

Question #9

How many times did the children of Israel march around Jericho?

   a)   1
   b)   6
   c)   7
   d)   13

Question #10

How many years did the children of Israel have to wander in the wilderness?

   a)   40
   b)   48
   c)   80
   d)   100

Numbers

ANSWERS

1. d) 4 (Acts 21:8–9)
2. c) 3,000 (Acts 2:1, 41)
3. c) 300 (Judges 15:4–5)
4. c) 430 (Exodus 12:40)
5. a) 300 (Judges 7:7)
6. c) 40 (Genesis 7:11–12)
7. d) 969 (Genesis 5:27)
8. d) 48 (Numbers 35:2, 7)
9. d) 13 (Joshua 6:1–4)
10. a) 40 (Numbers 14:27, 33)

Did you outsmart the Sunday schoolers?

Can You
Outsmart
a
Sunday
Schooler?

Here are some more questions left over from other categories, a little potpourri to test your general knowledge.

Question #1

When God told Jonah to go preach, where did Jonah flee to?

    a) Joppa
    b) Egypt
    c) Tarshish
    d) Rome

Question #2

The valley of the shadow of death is mentioned in what favorite psalm?

    a) 23
    b) 100
    c) 1
    d) 119

Question #3

When Satan tempted Jesus, what is the one place he didn't take Him?

    a) the wilderness
    b) the sea
    c) a mountain
    d) the temple

Question #4

The wilderness the children of Israel wandered in was called the wilderness of:

    a) Sin
    b) Kadesh Barnea
    c) Beersheba
    d) Jeruel

Question #5

How many people were on the ark during the flood?

    a) 2   c) 6
    b) 4   d) 8

Question #6

What is the only book of the Bible that mentions Lucifer?

    a) Revelation
    b) Isaiah
    c) Ezekiel
    d) Daniel

Question #7

What prophet saw the valley of dry bones?

    a) Ezekiel
    b) Elijah
    c) Elisha
    d) Ezra

Question #8

Who wrote most of the proverbs in the book
of Proverbs?

    a)   David
    b)   Solomon
    c)   Moses
    d)   Isaiah

Question #9

Who said, "I was glad when they said unto me,
Let us go into the house of the Lord"?

    a)   David
    b)   Moses
    c)   Solomon
    d)   Asaph

Question #10

Ecclesiastes 12:13 says the whole duty of man is to:

    a)   love the Lord with all your heart
    b)   love your neighbor as yourself
    c)   fear God and keep His commandments
    d)   remember now your Creator in the
          days of your youth

More Miscellany

ANSWERS

1. c) Tarshish (Jonah 1:1–3)

2. a) 23

3. b) the sea (Matthew 4:1–11)

4. a) Sin (Numbers 33:1, 12)

5. d) 8 (Genesis 6:10; 7:7)

6. b) Isaiah (Isaiah 14:12)

7. a) Ezekiel (Ezekiel 37:1)

8. b) Solomon (Proverbs 1:1)

9. a) David (Psalm 122:1)

10. c) fear God and keep His commandments

Did you outsmart the Sunday schoolers?

Can You
Outsmart
a
Sunday
Schooler?

There are many familiar couples in the Bible. Proverbs 18:22 says, "Whoso findeth a wife findeth a good thing." Some of the biblical couples we're familiar with show the truth of this verse. But some of them seem to defy this verse's logic. What do you know about the following husbands and wives?

Question #1

When David took Bathsheba, she was the wife of:

    a) Nathan   c) Uriah

    b) Zadok   d) Uzziah

Question #2

What wife helped trick her husband into giving his blessing to the wrong son?

    a) Rebekah

    b) Rachel

    c) Leah

    d) Jezebel

Question #3

Which of the following wives was *not* found by a well?

    a) Rebekah

    b) Rachel

    c) Bathsheba

    d) Zipporah

Question #4

Lot's wife was turned into a pillar of salt because:
- a) she refused to leave the city
- b) she was disrespectful to her husband
- c) she had committed adultery
- d) she looked back while the city was being destroyed

Question #5

What man's wife told him to curse God and die?
- a) Esau
- b) Job
- c) David
- d) Ishmael

Question #6

Priscilla and Aquila, who let Paul live with them, were:
- a) clothing makers
- b) tent makers
- c) cheese makers
- d) wine makers

Question #7

After David slew two hundred Philistines, King Saul gave his daughter _____ to David for a wife.
- a) Bathsheba
- b) Abigail
- c) Michal
- d) Tamar

Question #8

When Nabal churlishly refused to help David and his men, Nabal's wife, _____, interceded.

   a)   Abishag
   b)   Abigail
   c)   Tamar
   d)   Achish

Question #9

Who blamed his wife and God for a sin he committed?

   a)   David
   b)   Moses
   c)   Adam
   d)   Solomon

Question #10

What happened to Samson's first wife?

   a)   she died
   b)   she was given to another man
   c)   he divorced her
   d)   she refused to leave her father's house

Husbands and Wives

ANSWERS

1. c) Uriah (Matthew 1:6 NKJV)

2. a) Rebekah (Genesis 27:1–19)

3. c) Bathsheba (Genesis 24:10–16;
       29:9–10; Exodus 2:16–21)

4. d) she looked back while the city was
       being destroyed (Genesis 19:17, 26)

5. b) Job (Job 2:9)

6. b) tent makers (Acts 18:1–3)

7. c) Michal (1 Samuel 18:27)

8. b) Abigail (1 Samuel 25:14, 18–20,
       23–31)

9. c) Adam (Genesis 3:12)

10. b) she was given to another man
        (Judges 14:20)

Did you outsmart
the Sunday schoolers?

Can You
Outsmart
a
Sunday
Schooler?

Perhaps Paul was the apostle who had the most influence on the early church. God certainly used him mightily, especially to bring the gospel to the Gentiles. How much do you know about Paul's activities?

Question #1

How many books of the Bible did Paul write?

a) 1
b) 9
c) 12
d) 13

Question #2

Paul was a very educated man. To which group did he belong?

a) the Sadducees
b) the scribes
c) the Pharisees
d) the Sanhedrin

Question #3

How many days was Paul blind before God restored his sight?

a) 1
b) 2
c) 3
d) 4

Question #4

Paul wrote to Philemon concerning:
  a) a servant
  b) the law
  c) salvation
  d) grace

Question #5

Paul had a vision of a man from:
  a) Rome
  b) Macedonia
  c) Philippi
  d) Galatia

Question #6

Paul and Silas were beaten and put into prison in:
  a) Philippi
  b) Ephesus
  c) Colosse
  d) Rome

Question #7

Before Paul traveled with Silas, Paul traveled with:
  a) Peter
  b) Philip
  c) Barnabas
  d) Stephen

Question #8

Who said to Paul, "Almost thou persuadest me to be a Christian"?

- a) Festus
- b) Felix
- c) Agrippa
- d) Caesar

Question #9

When Paul was being tried, he appealed to:

- a) his fellow Christians
- b) Peter
- c) the church council
- d) Caesar

Question #10

The young man who fell out of the window when Paul was preaching was:

- a) Timothy
- b) Titus
- c) Eutychus
- d) John Mark

The Apostle Paul

ANSWERS

1. d) 13: Romans, 1 and 2 Corinthians, Galatians, Ephesians, Philippians, Colossians, 1 and 2 Thessalonians, 1 and 2 Timothy, Titus, Philemon. (Though the King James Bible ascribes Hebrews to Paul, Hebrews has no greeting from him, and from early on, scholars have not believed he penned this book.)

2. c) the Pharisees (Philippians 3:4–5)

3. c) 3 (Acts 9:8–9)

4. a) a servant (Philemon 10, 16)

5. b) Macedonia (Acts 16:9)

6. a) Philippi (Acts 16:12, 23–24)

7. c) Barnabas (Acts 13:2–3)

8. c) Agrippa (Acts 26:28)

9. d) Caesar (Acts 25:10–12)

10. c) Eutychus (Acts 20:9)

Did you outsmart the Sunday schoolers?

Can You
Outsmart
a
Sunday
Schooler?

Exodus 14:14 says, "The Lord shall fight for you, and ye shall hold your peace." While, indeed, all our battles are the Lord's, what do you know about these specific battles where God did all the fighting?

Question #1

In one of the battles that God fought for Joshua, God rained _____ down from heaven upon the enemy.

a) hail

b) stones

c) walls of water

d) fire

Question #2

What enemy was surrounding Jerusalem when the angel of the Lord smote and killed 185,000 men in one night?

a) the Philistines

b) the Babylonians

c) the Midianites

d) the Assyrians

Question #3

When Elisha's servant was afraid, Elisha prayed and the servant saw:

a) horses and chariots of fire

b) angels with swords

c) a huge dust cloud

d) a pillar of fire

Question #4

What was the last thing God had the children of Israel do before the walls of Jericho fell down?

a)   march around the city
b)   blow trumpets
c)   sing
d)   shout

Question #5

When the children of Israel fought the Amalekites, they won as long as Aaron and Hur:

a)   prayed
b)   offered sacrifices
c)   held up Moses' hands
d)   sang

Question #6

What king won a battle by sending singers instead of soldiers, as God had told him to do?

a)   Jehoshaphat
b)   Hezekiah
c)   Josiah
d)   Joash

Question #7

God told Moses that He would send what type of insects to drive out the Hivites, Canaanites, and Hittites?

a)   locusts
b)   hornets
c)   ants
d)   lice

Question #8

When Gideon did what God told him to do,
the battle was won because God:

- a) caused the enemy to kill one another
- b) sent chariots of fire to destroy
  the enemy
- c) washed the enemy away with a flood
- d) caused the earth to open up and
  swallow the enemy

Question #9

When the angels went to save Lot, they:

- a) struck the men of his city blind
- b) told Lot to get ready to leave
- c) led him out by the hand
- d) all of the above

Question #10

When God led the children of Israel out of Egypt,
how did He destroy the Egyptian army?

- a) by fire
- b) by water
- c) with hail
- d) the earth swallowed them

God's Battles

ANSWERS

1. b) stones (Joshua 10:5–11)

2. d) the Assyrians (2 Kings 19:35)

3. a) horses and chariots of fire
       (2 Kings 6:17)

4. d) shout (Joshua 6:1, 20)

5. c) held up Moses' hands
       (Exodus 17:10–12)

6. a) Jehoshaphat (2 Chronicles 20:1,
       21–22)

7. b) hornets (Exodus 23:28)

8. a) caused the enemy to kill one
       another (Judges 7:9–22)

9. d) all of the above (Genesis 19:1,
       11, 15–16)

10. b) by water (Exodus 14:26–30)

Did you outsmart
the Sunday schoolers?

Can You Outsmart a Sunday Schooler?

Many people in the Bible were filled with the Spirit of God, who empowered them to do great things for Him. Tragically, some, like King Saul and Samson, caused the Spirit to depart from them. But the following stayed true to their callings and were blessed. How much do you know about them?

Question #1

Bezalel was the person whom God handpicked and gave the skills to:

    a)   lead His army
    b)   write some of the Psalms
    c)   make the tabernacle
    d)   lead the temple singers

Question #2

God's Spirit came upon David when:

    a)   David played his harp
    b)   Samuel anointed him
    c)   David was crowned king
    d)   David killed Goliath

Question #3

Jesus said the Spirit of the Lord had anointed Him to:

    a)   preach
    b)   heal
    c)   liberate the oppressed
    d)   all of the above

Question #4

When the Spirit of the Lord came upon Zechariah, the son of Jehoiada, the people did not like what he said, so they:

    a) banished him
    b) stoned him
    c) drowned him
    d) buried him alive

Question #5

Elizabeth was filled with the Spirit, and when Mary greeted her:

    a) Elizabeth's baby leaped in her womb
    b) Elizabeth blessed Mary
    c) Elizabeth fixed Mary a meal
    d) both a and b

Question #6

Who said, "I was in the Spirit on the Lord's day"?

    a) John
    b) Peter
    c) Jesus
    d) Paul

Question #7

When the Holy Spirit was poured out on the Gentiles, the Jews:

    a) were dismayed
    b) were astonished
    c) didn't believe it
    d) didn't care

Question #8

One person asked for a double portion of the Spirit, and it was granted to him. That person was:

a) Elisha
b) Elijah
c) Isaiah
d) David

Question #9

Who was filled with the Spirit and saw Jesus standing at the right hand of God in heaven?

a) Paul
b) John
c) Stephen
d) Peter

Question #10

One list of the gifts of the Spirit is in 1 Corinthians:

a) 11
b) 12
c) 13
d) 14

Filled with the Spirit

ANSWERS

1. c) make the tabernacle
(Exodus 35:30–33 NKJV)

2. b) Samuel anointed him
(1 Samuel 16:13)

3. d) all of the above (Luke 4:18–19)

4. b) stoned him (2 Chronicles 24:20–21)

5. d) both a and b (Luke 1:41–42 NKJV)

6. a) John (Revelation 1:10)

7. b) were astonished (Acts 10:44–45)

8. a) Elisha (2 Kings 2:9)

9. c) Stephen (Acts 7:55)

10. b) 12

Did you outsmart
the Sunday schoolers?

Can You Outsmart a Sunday Schooler?

Christmas is one of the best-loved holidays of all. How much do you know about the real story of Christmas and the babe who was born to bring us all God's love?

Question #1

What verse in the Old Testament foretold that Jesus would be born in Bethlehem?

a) Isaiah 7:14
b) Micah 5:2
c) Isaiah 9:6–7
d) Joel 2:5

Question #2

Who was Caesar at the time Jesus was born?

a) Julius
b) Nero
c) Dominican
d) Augustus

Question #3

Which of the following women is *not* mentioned by name in Jesus' genealogy?

a) Rahab
b) Ruth
c) Bathsheba
d) Tamar (or Thamar)

Question #4

How old was Jesus when He was taken to the temple to be presented?

a) 1 day
b) 5 days
c) 7 days
d) 8 days

Question #5

What sacrifice was given for Jesus' presentation at the temple?

a) a lamb
b) a bullock
c) 2 turtledoves
d) a goat

Question #6

Whom did the wise men ask, "Where is he that is born King of the Jews?"

a) the shepherds
b) an angel
c) Herod
d) the priests

Question #7

Where did God tell Joseph to take Mary and Jesus to keep them safe?

a) Nazareth
b) Egypt
c) Jerusalem
d) Caesarea

Question #8

Herod ordered all the children in Bethlehem from the age of _____ and younger to be killed.

    a) 2 years
    b) 3 years
    c) 4 years
    d) 5 years

Question #9

Mary and Joseph went to Bethlehem to be registered because of:

    a) Herod
    b) a census
    c) a Roman law
    d) a desire to have their baby there

Question #10

The angels told the shepherds that the sign unto them would be:

    a) the star
    b) an angel
    c) the babe lying in a manger
    d) sheep grazing nearby

Nativity

ANSWERS

1. b) Micah 5:2
2. d) Augustus (Luke 2:1)
3. c) Bathsheba (Matthew 1:1–16)
4. d) 8 days (Luke 2:21–24)
5. c) 2 turtledoves (Luke 2:24)
6. c) Herod (Matthew 2:1–3)
7. b) Egypt (Matthew 2:13)
8. a) 2 years (Matthew 2:16)
9. b) a census (Luke 2:1–5)
10. c) the babe lying in a manger (Luke 2:8–12)

Did you outsmart the Sunday schoolers?

Can You
Outsmart
a
Sunday
Schooler?

Our God is an awesome God, and we need to give Him respect and awe for His wondrous works. The Bible is full of descriptions of God's glory.
Let us glorify our Lord together.

Question #1

Psalm 19:1 says, "The _____ declare the glory of God."

    a) worlds   c) heavens
    b) nations   d) people

Question #2

Romans 1:23 says man changed the glory of the incorruptible God into:

    a) an image of corruptible man
    b) birds
    c) creeping things
    d) all of the above

Question #3

When the tabernacle was finished and the glory of the Lord filled it, who could enter the tabernacle?

    a) the high priest
    b) no one
    c) Aaron
    d) Moses

Question #4

The glory of the Lord departed from Israel when:

a) the ark of the covenant was taken
b) they were taken into captivity
c) they refused to go into the Promised Land
d) they lost their battle

Question #5

When the glory of the Lord filled the temple Solomon built, the priests:

a) sacrificed a bull
b) had to leave
c) declared a feast
d) burned incense

Question #6

According to 1 Chronicles 16:24, we are to declare the Lord's glory to:

a) all people
b) each other
c) the heathen
d) the nations

Question #7

"For all have sinned, and come short of the glory of God" is found in:

a) Romans 3:23
b) Romans 4:23
c) Romans 5:23
d) Romans 6:23

Question #8

John says the people who saw Jesus beheld His glory, which was full of:

    a)   God's love
    b)   God's Spirit
    c)   grace and truth
    d)   goodness and truth

Question #9

The last part of the Lord's Prayer says God's glory is:

    a)   forever
    b)   everlasting
    c)   eternal
    d)   unending

Question #10

Psalm 24 says that God is the _____ of glory.

    a)   Lord
    b)   King
    c)   Prince
    d)   Author

God's Glory

ANSWERS

1. c) heavens
2. d) all of the above
3. b) no one (Exodus 40:35)
4. a) the ark of the covenant was taken
      (1 Samuel 4:17, 22)
5. b) had to leave (1 Kings 8:6, 10–11)
6. c) the heathen
7. a) Romans 3:23
8. c) grace and truth (John 1:14)
9. a) forever (Matthew 6:13)
10. b) King (Psalm 24:10)

Did you outsmart
the Sunday schoolers?